Red Leader is Missing

First published in 2025 by Patricia Salti,
in partnership with Andrew Crofts and Whitefox Publishing Ltd

www.wearewhitefox.com

Copyright © Patricia Salti, 2025

ISBN 978-1-917523-33-2
Also available as an eBook
ISBN 978-1-917523-34-9

EU GPSR Authorised Representative
LOGOS EUROPE, 9 rue Nicolas Poussin, 17000, LA ROCHELLE, France
E-mail: Contact@logoseurope.eu

Patricia Salti and Andrew Crofts assert the moral right to be identified as the authors of this work.

All rights reserved. No part of this publication may be reproduced, stored in a retrieval system or transmitted in any form or by any means, electronic, mechanical, photocopying, recording or otherwise, without prior written permission of the author.

While every effort has been made to trace the owners of copyright material reproduced herein, the author would like to apologise for any omissions and will be pleased to incorporate missing acknowledgements in any future editions.

All photographs in this book © Patricia Salti
Book cover painting of Qala'at ar-Rabadh, Ajlun by New Zealand artist Wendy Leach
(www.wendyleach.com)

Designed and typeset by Karen Lilje
Cover design by Michal Kuzmierkiewicz
Project management by Whitefox Publishing

PATRICIA SALTI
WITH ANDREW CROFTS

Red Leader is Missing

A Memoir

For Maia and Kiri

In memory of Lt Muwaffaq Salti RJAF (1939–1966)

This memoir reflects personal views and recollections based on the author's experiences at the time and should not be viewed as verified historical fact.

He left me at dawn with love
His child within me
The sirens went and off he flew
Never to come back
What a waste of life war is
And for what?

Contents

Prologue xiii

1. In Search of a Great Adventure 1
2. Driving into the Unknown 11
3. The Expat Lifestyle 15
4. Fighter Pilots 25
5. 'Don't Kiss Me Here' 35
6. Extended Family 43
7. Red Leader is Missing 55
8. Returning with Baby Muwaffaq 81
9. Working for the King 91
10. Refugee Wives 101
11. Life in England 109
12. Help from the King 119
13. Becoming an Activist 131
14. Women and Children 139
15. The Death of the King 149
16. Discoveries in the Dead Sea 153
17. A Return Trip 157

Acknowledgements 161

Prologue

Extract from the No. 1 Squadron Diary of the Royal Jordanian Air Force

Sunday November 13, 1966
It was a lovely morning and at 0700 hours everybody was in the squadron on duty. Our OC flying was giving a briefing when a phone call came through reporting heavy activity over Hebron area. All operational pilots were called and two minutes later it was 'SCRAMBLE', everybody rushed to the aircraft and eventually Salti and Shurdom got airborne, followed later by Jasser and Farouk. All other pilots were trying to find a serviceable aircraft to strap in. Some even were strapped in while bowsers were filling the aircraft. Few moments later it heard that Red Section, Salti and Shurdom engaged. Blue Section was almost in the area and they engaged also. Hearing that a third pair was scrambled, Smadi and Shiyab also the fourth pair Matta and Najjar started up with short range aircraft and empty outer tanks. But they were held at the marshalling points when all of a sudden Blue Section returned followed shortly afterwards by Red 2 Shurdom alone. Blue Section claimed two Mirage III's, Red 2 when asked about his leader said that he heard him coming back. Around 0930 hours everybody was back on ground except for Red Leader. Talking about the combat Red 2 said that he split from his leader and fired at a Mirage but wasn't sure of a kill. Blue Section claimed one Mirage each and at one stage heard him calling 'Help, somebody do something'.

From later reports the combat looked something like four Mirages to one Hunter. Blue Leader reported a missile being fired at Red 2, also he reported Red Leader calling 'Hunter behind Mirage, break, break'. Also he reported him saying that he will be crossing the Dead Sea and he changed to 'G' Golf.

So far Red Leader is missing and was overdue. Shurdom reported on his way back 2 Mirages in the Dead Sea area also he reported seeing what looked like an explosion near the sea shore.

With great sorrow and grief we record here the death of one of our most proficient pilots, Lieutenant M. B. Salti. No tribute will be enough for such a great pilot and a good friend. May he rest in peace. And so with the loss of Salti, the RJAF lost its first pilot who gave his life fighting for the honour of his country. Standby was on all day. Besides that, four aircraft flew an escort for President Ayub Khan of Pakistan on his state visit to Jordan.

I

In Search of a Great Adventure

I WAS NOT SURPRISED to hear about the attack on Israel from Gaza on 7 October 2023. Saddened, horrified and disgusted, of course, but not surprised. Nor was I surprised by the ferocious, genocidal response that the Israeli government launched on the citizens of Gaza in the following months, and the widening attacks on the West Bank and Lebanon after that. When stories started to come out about mass rapes on 7 October, beheadings and the burning of babies, I remembered how much the Israelis had lied in the past and found it hard to believe anything they said now. I was amazed that Hamas managed to inflict as much damage as they had with their attack and suspected that they were also surprised by their own success. It seems from the evidence that the Israelis completely misread the situation and made grave errors. Maybe one day historians will be able to find their way through all the propaganda coming from every side and understand how such an attack was possible. Who knows what will have happened to the Palestinians in Gaza, and the wider Middle East by the time that happens.

I have the most personal reasons in the world for holding the strong opinions that I do on the subject. I am the widow of a Jordanian martyr and have been for nearly sixty years. I am in my eighties, but I march in London at every opportunity, to protest at what is happening now, and has been happening since the 1930s. My life was punctuated by a great tragedy, but either side of that tragedy I have lived as full a life as I think could have been possible for an English woman of my generation. I have taken many risks, some of which others might consider foolish, some of which were mistakes, but most of which have allowed me to lead a rich and varied life and given me the opportunity to see the world from more than one perspective. As a single mother and long-term expatriate, I have lived precariously in many ways, becoming entangled with a royal dynasty, moving between war zones and palaces and travelling naively on a variety of dangerous roads.

It started out as a great adventure, a journey to a country and a culture I knew nothing about and a future no one could have predicted, least of all me, an English girl from a sheltered background. Perhaps, if I had foreseen what lay in store for me, I would never have plucked up the courage to even start the journey. The ignorance of youth can sometimes provide a shield against fear, particularly when you are eager to escape from the mundane and ordinary life which you fear you may be destined for.

I hadn't excelled at school. I wasn't hopeless, I just didn't shine at anything. I didn't catch the academic bug and I felt no great urge to follow any sort of higher educational route. It was the beginning of the 1960s, when the scars of the Second World War were starting to fade in Britain and many things were changing, particularly for my generation, who were just coming of age, and also for women who wanted more from life than marriage and motherhood. Upon leaving school, my parents, wanting me to have something solid to fall back on if I wasn't going to follow a recognised profession of any sort, persuaded me to follow the most traditional route of all and take a secretarial course. The fact that the college was in the centre of London made it a more tempting prospect than it might otherwise have been. London at that time had a reputation for being the most 'swinging' city in the

West and seemed to promise all sorts of possibilities for adventure. The course taught me some useful skills and I could see that being a secretary would be a good way of ensuring that I always had an income, but the thought of spending the rest of my life in offices and typing pools, churning out letters for other people, was not attractive.

After a year studying in London, I returned to the family home in Wolverhampton and took a job as a secretary to the personnel director at a local factory. I really didn't want to live at home, but on a salary of £10 a week there wasn't much choice. The factory, which was part of the Courtauld Group and produced tyre yarn, was a good experience for a first job, but I certainly didn't want to spend any longer there than I had to. I yearned for travel, excitement and new experiences, but had no idea how to go about attaining them without money.

My parents were both broad-minded for the time, though they came from two very different backgrounds. My father was born in India during the time of British colonialism. His father, my grandfather, worked on the Indian railways between Calcutta and Lucknow, and my father was despatched to boarding school in the cool hills of northern India for nine months a year from the age of four and a half, a separation from his parents which must have been hard for him and my grandmother. At the age of ten he was shipped even further away, to a boarding school in England, but he maintained a love of India all his life, and kept up with a number of his Indian friends. He met and married my mother during the Second World War while he was serving in the army as a 'boffin', having studied aeronautical engineering at university. He didn't see active service and left the army in the 1950s for the commercial world, starting off in consultancy, which meant moving around a lot. We lived in Ireland for a bit while he managed a nylon factory. He then joined the famous Chubb & Sons Lock and Safe Company. Later, he became Chairman of the Chubb Fire & Security

Group and, just before his death at the age of sixty-two, he received the OBE.

My mother came from a family that had little money. Her father went bankrupt after trying to run his own business and then left to live with another woman, so my mother, despite being very smart, didn't have the chance to receive a full education, instead leaving school at the age of fourteen in order to earn a living and contribute to the family coffers.

I was the eldest of their three daughters and they must have worried that my restless nature would lead me into trouble. My sister Jill, who later became a GP, was four years younger than me. Ann, who was eleven years younger, married a British Airways pilot, studied for a law degree and eventually became a magistrate and does other voluntary work as well. Both of them followed much safer and more sensible paths through life.

One evening my parents came home from a dinner party and told me about how their host's daughter had applied for a job at the Foreign Office and was now being posted abroad.

My ears immediately pricked up. The idea of being sent 'abroad' was extremely tantalising and given that I had now acquired some secretarial experience, it didn't seem unreasonable to think that if I applied to join the Foreign Office, I might be accepted. The other major stipulation for any woman wishing to join the service at that time was that she should be unmarried. If she did become betrothed, she would immediately have to hand in her notice. Since I was still only twenty years old, and had yet to have any significant romantic entanglement, I could also tick that box. The men, of course, were perfectly free to marry. Equal employment rights for women were still a long way off, but like most of my gender at that time I accepted this systemic misogyny without any great complaint or indignation and dreamed of a posting to some exotic, faraway destination.

Up until then my experience of travel was limited to family holidays in Devon, or the recently invented 'package holidays' in places like Mallorca and Ibiza. Those short trips to the sun had been enough to whet my appetite for new and foreign experiences. Up until the invention of the package holiday, travel had really been the preserve of those rich enough to afford time off work, as well as expensive tickets and hotels. Ordinary people generally only left England if they were part of the colonial services, (like my grandfather, working on the Indian railway) fighting in a foreign war or working in international business. The only knowledge most of us had about other countries came from books by writers who had been lucky enough to get out and experience other worlds.

My application was accepted. My grown-up life was about to start.

•

As I had joined for an overseas posting, I had to undergo a minimum of six weeks' training in London before I would be told where I was going. So, initially, the adventure was to start at the Foreign Office in Westminster, at the very heart of the British government. Every day I would be walking past Downing Street, (there were no gates or security guards in those days, just a solitary policeman, if my memory serves me), past awe-inspiring buildings and statues, into the labyrinthine corridors and echoing staircases of the Foreign Office, which seemed to be almost entirely staffed by pompous old asses and brash young public schoolboys. That, at least, was how it felt to me and the other young women whose duties were largely to make tea and take dictation from men with plummy voices. We couldn't help but wonder if we were destined to become like the older women who remained, unmarried, in the Foreign Office all their working lives.

The atmosphere of colonialism and Empire lingered everywhere and the certainty that the British were naturally superior to the rest of the world and the best at everything permeated all our work. Every day I felt like I was walking through and with history. Throughout the coldest months of the winter, I travelled up daily from an aunt's house in Croydon on a crowded commuter train full of wordless men in suits and ties reading newspapers. I don't think I could have stood (literally) more than six weeks of this travelling torture.

At the end of our training period, we were asked which part of the world we would like to go to and all I could think of was that it should be 'somewhere warm'. Unlike most Foreign Office recruits, I didn't hanker to be sent to one of the big embassies, like Washington, Bonn or Paris. I yearned for somewhere more exotic, a leap into the unknown. Perhaps there was a distant echo in my soul from my father's colonial childhood.

When I was told that I was to be posted to the embassy in the Hashemite Kingdom of Jordan, I headed straight to the library to find out where it was in an atlas. All I knew was that it was somewhere in the Middle East and was ruled by King Hussein. I think I might also have heard of Glubb Pasha, the British soldier who had trained and led the Arab Legion, but I had never met an Arab myself and had only a stereotypical romantic vision in my mind of a Bedouin living in his tent in the desert, riding around on his camel. Two of the girls at secretarial school had actually been expelled after they were caught 'mixing with Arabs', (the Bayswater area, where the school was situated, was popular with visitors from the Middle East) an alien species that we 'nice' British girls were told we should have nothing to do with, for fear, perhaps, that we would be kidnapped and whisked off into the desert as 'white slaves'. All these warnings, of course, served only to make the men and the far-off world they came from more interesting to me.

There were plenty of exotic-sounding facts to be found in reference books, none of which really told me what to prepare for. Jordan, I discovered, was in the Southern Levant region of West Asia, bordered by the equally exotic-sounding Syria, Iraq, Saudi Arabia and Israel, with a small coastline along the Red Sea, separated by the Gulf of Aqaba from Egypt. The Jordan river flowed through the country into the Dead Sea. Amman, where the British embassy stood and where I would be based, was the country's capital city.

Further research revealed a bit more history of the country I would live in for forty-one years. In 1921, Emir Abdullah bin al-Hussein (Abdullah I), of the Hashemite family established the Emirate of Transjordan. The Hashemites are direct descendants of the Prophet Muhammad, who lived between 570 and 632, through his daughter, Fatima. Their descendant, Sharif Hussein bin Ali, the emir of Mecca, (great-great grandfather of Abdullah II, the current king of Jordan) initiated the Arab Revolt against the Turks in 1916, in alliance with the Allies against the Ottoman Empire, an event best remembered in Britain through the adventures of 'Lawrence of Arabia'. Sharif Hussein's sons, Abdullah (later King Abdullah I of Jordan), Faisal (later King of Iraq) and Zeid, led the Arab forces to success.

At the end of the Great War, Transjordan came under a British mandate and by 1921 Abdullah was the ruler. In 1946 the country became a fully independent and sovereign state and Abdullah was proclaimed King. In 1917 the British promised, in the Balfour Declaration, to support the establishment of a Jewish 'national home' in Palestine. The Mandate for Palestine was established in 1920 and the British obtained it from the League of Nations in 1922. When the British forces eventually withdrew from Palestine in 1948, they left behind a complete void and the Arab Legion, under the command of Glubb Pasha, moved from the East Bank of Jordan to defend as much of the land as possible. With a few brave personnel, and not much ammunition, they managed to hang on to what is now called the West Bank and East Jerusalem, which was subsequently lost to Israel in 1967.

Glubb's wonderful book, *A Soldier with the Arabs*, paints a vivid picture of those brutal times.

King Abdullah 1 was assassinated in Jerusalem on 20 July 1951 while attending Friday prayers at Al-Aqsa Mosque. He was succeeded by his son Talal, who later abdicated due to ill health, leading to King Hussein coming to the throne on 11 August 1952.

•

Suffice to say this was exactly the sort of plunge into the unknown that I had been dreaming of. No more factories in rainy Wolverhampton for me.

I decided that the best way to get to my new job, 3,000 miles away from London, would be to drive there, since the journey would be mostly overland. So, with the help of a loan from the Foreign Office, I bought myself a brand-new Mini Traveller. Compared to today's cars, Minis, which had only been on the market a few years by then, were very basic and not particularly comfortable, but when you are twenty-one years old and embarking on a great adventure, comfort is not something you worry too much about. This way, I reasoned, the journey would be an adventure in itself.

Surprisingly, my parents raised no objections to any of these highly risky plans. I can only think that the Middle East was such an unknown quantity to them, they didn't worry about their eldest daughter heading off on her own quite as much as they might have done if they had known more about what potential hazards lay in store. As it turned out, I didn't set off alone, because I met Alice, another girl at the Foreign Office, who was being sent to Baghdad. We decided to travel together as far as Beirut. Alice couldn't drive, however, so I was still going to be doing that on my own. Although my parents were very relaxed about the whole thing, they must have wondered if they would ever see me again as they waved me off to catch the ferry to Europe and on into the unknown. Or perhaps they assumed I would find the whole thing overwhelming and come scurrying back to England and a safer future once I had exorcised the wanderlust from my soul.

2

Driving into the Unknown

ALICE AND I BOARDED the cross-channel ferry with barely a backwards glance at the white cliffs of Dover. As we emerged onto the deck to enjoy the salty wind on our faces, we were bubbling with excitement at the adventures we felt sure lay ahead of us. That excitement built with the clanking of chains and the shouts of ferry workers as we disembarked in France, and then we were off, on the other side of the road, our hearts in our mouths.

Driving across France and Italy in April, just as spring was breaking through along the verges and in the gardens and window boxes of the villages we passed, banished all thoughts of tiredness or nervousness. Each day we would set off early and then, as evening approached, we would search for small hotels in which to lay our heads. Not being experienced map-readers, we became lost on several occasions but we kept ploughing on, in what we hoped was the right direction, enjoying each day as it came.

The scenery grew progressively more beautiful and the air progressively warmer as we drove south. Despite our occasional deviations, we completed the 800-mile trip from Calais to Genoa along the Italian Riviera a full two days before the ship we were booked on was due to leave for Beirut, via Alexandria.

We could now relax and with time on our hands we were able to take in the sights of the city and linger pleasantly in modest restaurants, drinking in the atmosphere and chatting, as best we could, with locals. It wasn't long before Alice was picked up by a charming Italian man who decided, after two days in her company, that she was the one woman in all the world he wanted to marry. He begged her not to sail out of his life so soon after meeting him and, to my amazement, she seemed to be contemplating his offer with great seriousness. I managed to dissuade her from settling so readily for the first man outside England who asked for her hand, but he continued his campaign to persuade her all the way down to the docks. When we had finally succeeded in manoeuvring the car and ourselves onboard and up on deck, we could still see and hear her abandoned Romeo on the dockside, plaintively calling out her name in the hope that she would relent at the last moment and run back down the gangplank into his arms. I was extremely relieved when the ship finally hauled up the ramps and churned slowly away from the dock out into the Ligurian Sea.

Alice's mildly broken heart was soon mended by some wonderfully handsome Iranian men who flirted with us throughout the voyage, although there were no offers of marriage this time. It was all a long way from the patronising and unromantic middle-class Englishmen we had been surrounded by in Whitehall. It seemed that life was going to be very different for us in these sunnier climes.

We sailed down to the Mediterranean, past Sardinia and Corsica, around Sicily and on to Alexandria and Beirut. After Lebanon gained independence from the French in 1943, Beirut, one of the oldest cities in the world, became its capital, famed for its intellectual life and a popular tourist destination and banking centre. It had a beautiful corniche, sparkling blue seas and lush mountains in the background. The people we met at the British embassy told us that it was extremely hot and humid in the summer, which made it quite uncomfortable, but it was still an exciting and sophisticated place to be. This was more than a decade before the Lebanese Civil War broke out and the city became infamous for being a dangerous war zone, the scene of many bombings, shootings and kidnappings. We were lucky to experience it at the peak of its cosmopolitan glamour.

In Beirut, Alice and I parted company, she to make her way to Baghdad, I to travel the 200 miles on to Amman. I met up with an English couple who had also been posted to the embassy in Amman, so we drove down in convoy, which I was grateful for, not relishing the idea of being entirely alone on strange roads in a part of the world where I knew absolutely nothing of the language or local customs.

We set off early in the morning, climbing the stunningly beautiful hills of Lebanon and dropping down into Damascus, the oldest current capital in the world, believed by some to be the fourth holiest city in Islam. As we drove through Syria, however, everything started to look very different. The heat was rising, necessitating the opening of the car windows and I felt increasingly uneasy at the sight of the dirt and poverty amidst the shacks that lined the roads. Was I going to be expected to live like this? Would I be able to cope with such squalor? The Syrian border post at Dera'a was a chaotic nightmare of jostling people, all shouting at the tops of their voices, pushing and shoving to get their passports stamped by the bored-looking and unhelpful officials. After what seemed like hours, we finally got past all the border hassles and drove through to the Jordanian side. By then it was late afternoon and I dreaded the thought of wasting more hours, and more nervous energy, on another difficult crossing. It would be dark before we reached Amman and I was worried about driving on the terrible, pot-holed, unlit roads we had been experiencing thus far in Syria. Adventures that seem so exciting in the planning stages and are so pleasantly nostalgic to look back on in hindsight can be very frightening at the time of their unfolding when you have no idea what lies around the next corner and when there is absolutely no chance of turning back and heading for home.

Arriving at Ramtha, however, I felt my spirits rise once more. This was nothing like the Syrian crossing. The Jordanian soldiers were smartly dressed and friendly, our passports and papers were efficiently processed and we were through to the other side in no time. Dusk was falling as we drove down to Jerash, with cat's eyes blinking in the middle of the smooth, winding road. I felt my optimism rising once more and the dread receding. If the Jordanians have cat's eyes in their roads, I thought, maybe everything will be all right after all.

I was due to spend my first night in Amman at the apartment of the ambassador's personal assistant who, not knowing I would be arriving that evening, had gone partying down by the Dead Sea. So, once I had taken leave of my fellow travellers, I found myself on my own at the end of the long journey and my spirits plummeted once more. I suddenly felt lonely, dislocated and far from home. I had not realised quite how cold the Middle East could be at night. Knowing nobody and having nothing to do, I went to bed absolutely frozen, even though it was the end of April and it had been a hot, sticky drive down from Beirut.

Was this really the Middle East? The land of deserts and burning sun? Had I made a terrible mistake?

3

The Expat Lifestyle

THE NEXT MORNING THE warmth of the sun had returned and I woke to discover that Amman was a picturesque city with houses constructed of white and pink limestone clinging to the sides of the seven *jebels* (hills), with the sounds of the call to prayer reverberating around the hills. I climbed out of bed and got myself dressed in preparation for my first day in the new job. The sounds and smells of the busy streets between the apartment and the embassy as the city went about its daily life were just as unfamiliar and alluring as I had dreamed they would be. I felt a heady mix of excitement and trepidation at the strangeness all around me.

The layout of the city was puzzling. The main residential hill was Jebel Amman, defined by roundabouts that everyone called 'circles'. It started off at the first circle and ended at the third where the British embassy was located. I soon learned that if you were invited to someone's house, directions would start at a circle, since most streets had no names. We would say: 'turn left at the third circle, then right at the pharmacy on the corner, then two doors along from the small grocery shop', which would then find us in the right place. As the years went by, with urbanisation and development, the streets were given names and the number of circles increased to eight. Now, they are mostly ruled by traffic lights, but we still refer to them by their circle numbers, which can be very confusing to newcomers. Today, Amman has spread out in many different directions and it is almost impossible to give anyone directions, even though the streets have names.

Wherever people were building or repairing houses, you would hear the chipping sound of the stonemasons, sitting on their haunches, shaping piles of limestone rocks into building materials, along with the incessant hooting of the pick-up trucks full of gas cylinders, which drove everyone so crazy it was eventually stopped. Then you would see and hear the flocks of sheep and goats with bells around their necks, wandering through the streets, feeding themselves in any empty plots of land they came across.

I would gradually learn about the difficulties of living in Amman, as well as the pleasures. Water, for instance, was always in short supply, even when the population was still relatively small. Now that the city has swelled to about two million souls, the problem is even more acute. Hopefully, it would arrive once a week, pumped into a water tank on the roof, but sometimes it could be up to six weeks between flows into the system, so then one had to call for a water tanker to make a special delivery. If you lived near a hospital or a royal residence, however, the water came every day. I was always conscious of saving water even while brushing my teeth, and I still do it now. Once a habit has become ingrained it is hard to shake it off.

The population of Amman in 1964 was about 284,000 and seemed to me to be mostly middle class, with a few rich people. Although there was undoubtedly poverty, the city gave the general impression of bustling prosperity. I would eventually learn that there were many underlying social problems, but at that stage they didn't affect me because working at the embassy automatically endowed me with a privileged position in society. As in most cities, it was all too easy for the 'haves' of Amman to go through life with no contact at all with the 'have-nots'. Outside the city, the poverty was more obvious, because life in the desert is harsh in the extreme and there are none of the comforts of shops and restaurants, homes and hotels, to offer respite.

In 1964 Jordan was a larger country than it is now (as the West Bank was part of the Hashemite Kingdom), with a society made up of nomadic and settled Bedouins, urban Palestinians, refugee Palestinians from 1948, as well as Circassians and Armenians with their unique cultures and traditions. Only about 6 per cent of the population were Christians.

I was eager to meet people from as many different backgrounds as possible. As I got to know people from all walks of life in the coming months, I learned more of their subtle cultural differences. The Palestinians seemed to me to be sophisticated, with an entrepreneurial flair, in contrast to the rather more serious people of the East Bank. There was a great deal of mistrust between the two. The East Bank Jordanians did indeed rule the country, while the West Bank Jordanians took care of the business side of things. The government employees and the armed forces were mostly Jordanian, whereas the Palestinians seemed more international in their outlook. That was how I saw it at the time and I guess I received my initial opinions from those working around me at the embassy.

To quote the British ambassador in 1964, in a despatch to the Foreign Office:

> 'Over the past ten years the more sophisticated and enterprising West Bankers have penetrated Amman, and the catalyst effect their advent has had on the more conservative East Bankers has resulted in the overall impression of a city of sturdy individuals, each determined to educate his children and raise himself by his economic bootstraps. Palestinians and Trans-Jordanians are two distinct races. The Palestinian smooth and relatively subtle,

essentially a Mediterranean, the Trans-Jordanian dour and unimaginative, the product of his own deserts. Little real fusion has taken place and, ethnically speaking, the Jordanian does not exist. There is mutual suspicion even, I fear, a basic dislike: no East Banker trusts a West Banker and vice versa. The West Banker is more mature, if a trifle flabby, and the tougher East Banker runs the country.'

The embassy had allocated me a two-bedroom apartment with a nice balcony. I was one of around five single girls working there, which gave me a ready-made group of friends with whom to explore the city and the countryside, filled with ancient monuments, and through whom I could meet other people. It was great to have the freedom of my car, but the Mini turned out to be less than ideal as I could hardly use it during the heat of summer due to its transverse engine, which caused it to overheat, always at the most inconvenient times. Driving to Jerusalem and the West Bank on a hot, sunny day could sometimes take us hours. It was all right going downhill into the Jordan Valley, but climbing up the other side was just too much for it and the engine constantly emitted clouds of steam as the radiator boiled over, forcing us to stop to allow it to cool and refill the water. I often felt suffocated by the heat myself, so it wasn't just the car that needed plenty of water. The Mini was better, however, than the ancient Volkswagen Beetle that one of the guys working for the British Bank of the Middle East owned. This car had no petrol gauge, making every journey with him full of suspense, since he could never remember when he had last filled it up.

Although I was by now an experienced driver, the roads could be nerve-racking and I seemed to avoid accidents more by luck than judgement. One evening, however, my luck ran out. I was driving with Liz, one of the other girls from the embassy, up the hill towards the Third Circle when I was blinded by a car coming down with its headlights on full beam, something all the local drivers seemed to do. Looking to the side of the road for a few seconds so that I could refocus my eyes, I didn't see a woman dashing out from behind the oncoming car. She ran straight into me, hitting the left side of the Mini and falling dramatically. Liz and I jumped out of the car and found her lying, bleeding, on the road. Within seconds a huge crowd had gathered around us and the woman was bundled into a taxi, amidst much angry shouting and gesticulating, to be rushed to hospital. I was in shock. It was the first time I had ever had an accident and the crowd was frighteningly hostile towards me. In Jordan, I soon discovered, whatever the situation and circumstances, the driver is always at fault in an accident. Even if someone fell from a fourth-floor window onto the roof of a parked car, the driver could be held responsible. There was even more anger and aggression in their raised voices because I was both a foreigner and a woman. We eventually managed to get to a nearby police station where they could see how distressed I was and took pity on me.

'I have never seen anyone cry so much,' one of the policemen told me, as he tried to reassure me that I wasn't going to be lynched by the mob.

Following a garbled phone call, someone from the embassy came to my rescue and I was allowed home, but a court case followed. Luckily, I was going so slowly – in third gear, up a hill and in a Mini – that there could be no accusation of reckless driving, but I still felt terrible. I visited the woman in hospital, where she stayed for about a week. I think she was a maid to one of the princesses. It was a frightening introduction to the rules, laws and traditions that were very different to anything I would have expected if the incident had occurred in England. In the court, for instance, I was sitting meekly in front of the judge with my legs crossed. The translator requested that I uncross them, as the judge didn't 'want to see me like that'. I had no idea that such a small thing could be considered disrespectful. Every day was a learning experience.

Up until 1968 there was no local television in Jordan, which didn't bother me, but those who couldn't do without the square box would erect makeshift Eiffel-like towers on their roofs that worked as aerials so that they could receive programmes from Lebanon. There used to be regular flights from RAF Cyprus, which would occasionally bring a film to show on an outdoor screen and also some nice Cypriot wine. Sean Connery as James Bond in *Dr. No* was one film I particularly remember watching, sitting under the stars on a balmy night.

I found the weather in Amman to be nearly ideal. Middle Eastern summers are inevitably hot, but the city's height gave it more of a desert climate, which meant hot days and a considerable drop in temperature at night. Even at the peak of summer, it was wise to take a cardigan or wrap when going out at night, unless you were in the Jordan Valley where it was always boiling hot. I had been there some months before I discovered that the winters can be cold, wet and sometimes even snowy. There would be many a year I would find myself marooned at home, struggling to keep warm.

I hated the kerosene heaters that we used, they were such messy things. Large cans of kerosene had to be hauled upstairs and which always seemed to slop all over the place, especially when I was attempting to refill the small cylinders. To heat bathwater, there was a long, circular tank, which needed a wood fire to be lit underneath it and then continually stoked up until the water was hot. It all seemed primitive in the extreme and although this added to the sense of adventure to start with, it soon became very tiresome. Now, of course, many homes in Amman have central heating.

Cooking was done on a stove, using a gas cylinder as there was, and still is, no mains gas in the city. A family would change their cylinder about once every fortnight, but as I was not an enthusiastic cook, mine always lasted for months. My growing circle of friends and acquaintances were exceptionally diligent in making sure that I was well-fed.

The embassy was a small one, situated at the Third Circle in the residential area. The ambassador, Sir Roderick Parkes, was a character and I did think him rather an old-fashioned Brit at the time. It is only recently that I have discovered, after reading many of the reports on Jordanian society that he sent to London in the early 1960s, that he was an extremely astute and witty man. These reports make fascinating reading, especially after more than sixty years have elapsed. Many of his observations still hold good today.

'Rumours are rampant,' he wrote in one despatch, 'a popular pastime ... whilst the motives of leading personalities, already obscure and twisted enough to satisfy the most ardent psychologist, are mulled over with inexhaustible enthusiasm in coffee shops and private homes alike. Small wonder that King Hussein named his autobiography *Uneasy Lies the Head*.'

•

I dare say the present ambassador could write exactly the same words today, and probably does.

Sir Roderick and Lady Parkes lived in a lovely house in the palace complex, which is situated on a jebel opposite the Roman theatre in downtown Amman. It was built in an Arab style, with courtyards and vaulted ceilings. Their garden was the most beautiful in Jordan, and probably still is. Since the late 1960s it has been the home of the brother of King Hussein, Prince Hassan and his wife Princess Sarvath, both of whom I would work for in later years when Hassan was the crown prince.

At the embassy, I was one of two people working for the diplomats who weren't on the intelligence or military side and the work was boring in the extreme. I still hated typing and although my shorthand was excellent, as soon as I sat in front of the typewriter my grasp of language deteriorated in alarming proportion to the number of mistakes made. Making matters worse, all my worst mistakes seemed to come just as I reached the bottom of the page. There would then be my frantic attempts at rubbing out the error, often ending with a hole in the fifth copy, which would necessitate ripping the offending report out of the typewriter, carefully preserving the carbons, then tearing the paper into as many pieces as I could. I was ashamed of my full rubbish bin at the end of each day. Stencils were even worse, as the evidence of my carelessness showed in the mass of bright pink spots covering the mistakes.

We worked from eight in the morning until two in the afternoon, five days a week, so that we could avoid the hottest part of the day. We came back to the embassy in the late afternoon on 'bag day', when the diplomatic courier flew in with all the confidential papers from London and then left with all our confidential papers. Although I had nothing to do with intelligence, I was quite surprised at the criticisms of Jordanian personalities sent back to England, which often had a lethal sting.

Although the work was boring, I loved everything else about my life in and around the city once I had settled in. There wasn't much of a nightlife scene, only a few nightclubs and pubs. Jordanians mainly relied on their extended families for their social lives, so those of us who worked at the embassy, along with other expats who didn't have families in Jordan, would spend most of our weekends exploring the country together. It is a land of dramatic contrasts, from the deserts of the south and east, to the green and mountainous areas of the north and down to the Great Rift Valley. When I arrived, the West Bank was part of the kingdom, which meant that we could easily drive to the wonderful old towns of Hebron, Nablus, Ramallah, Jericho and,

Jordan's greatest jewel, the Old City of Jerusalem, for days out. Now, the West Bank is no longer easily accessible from Jordan, as it is occupied by Israel, so it is the 'rose red' city of Petra, the ancient Roman city of Jerash, the UNESCO world heritage site of Salt, the incredible Wadi Rum, the desert castles and many other ancient and natural wonders that continue to draw tourists to a very differently shaped Jordan.

My life became a never-ending round of socialising, from embassy cocktail parties to horse-riding at the polo ground or swimming at the InterContinental hotel and then trying to catch up on lost sleep. For someone who had lived quite a narrow life in England, with absolutely no social confidence, to be suddenly thrust into this hectic world of gatherings and outings, meeting so many new and fascinating people, was thrilling stuff. Being single, foreign girls meant we were very much in favour with all the men, Jordanian and other nationalities. And then, to top it all off, I was introduced to the King and his fighter pilots at the go-kart track.

4

Fighter Pilots

KING HUSSEIN, A DIRECT descendant of the Prophet Muhammad, forty generations removed, cut a charismatic figure. He had ascended to the throne in 1952 at the age of seventeen after a short reign by his father, who had become King himself only a year before, following the assassination of his own father, King Abdullah I, at Al-Aqsa Mosque in Jerusalem. Young Prince Hussein had actually been standing at his grandfather's side when the fatal bullet struck him.

Go-karting happened every Friday afternoon at Marka, close to the airfield that was used both as an air force base and as the international airport. King Hussein and Princess Muna (his second wife, a lovely English woman) were often there with their two small sons, Abdullah and Faisal, along with friends and some of the air force pilots. As well as enjoying fast cars, King Hussein was a keen aviator and enjoyed the company of his heroic fighter pilots.

As part of my initial briefing, the embassy had warned me not to get mixed up with the Royal Jordanian Air Force (RJAF) pilots as they were having a problem at that time with one who had married an English girl in the UK then returned alone to Jordan, leaving his pregnant wife behind. After a lot of hassle, she finally joined him, but the warning was there. In fact, there were about six English wives in the air force at that time, and more in the army, but that situation was about to be officially curtailed. Many Jordanian men who left the country to study overseas brought back foreign wives when they came home, often to the horror of their families. Doctors were especially vulnerable to falling in love with and marrying foreign women as they could spend up to seven years studying abroad, with very few trips back home in-between. I imagine the more liberated attitudes of Western women were just as novel and exciting for these dashing Arab men as the men were to the girls.

One day, as I was leaving the InterContinental hotel after using the swimming pool, I bumped into one of the pilots I had met at the go-karting.

'Would you like to go for a drive with me?' he asked.

'Yes,' I replied, not thinking twice about ignoring the embassy's advice, 'that would be nice.'

'I just have to pass by a friend for a minute to pick up something,' he said.

Only later did I discover that this 'something' was money, about £4-worth of Jordanian dinars, as he was broke at the time. So we went on our first date on borrowed money and oh, how nice he was. His name, I discovered, was Muwaffaq (which means 'successful') Salti. He was very dark-skinned, with a lovely face and he was the eldest son in a family of eight children, which was a position that carried a lot of prestige. In Arab families, the father and mother take on the name of their eldest son so his parents were known as Abu ('Father of') Muwaffaq and Umm ('Mother of') Muwaffaq.

He had spent two years in the UK, training with the Royal Air Force, and had received his wings there in 1962. Like so many of his peers, he actually got engaged to a girl while he was in England but, luckily for me, the relationship had not worked out and he was still single. Upon his return to Jordan, he was stationed at the King Hussein Air Base, near the village of Mafraq in northern Jordan. He flew Hunter jets, the transonic fighter aircraft developed by Hawker Aircraft for the RAF (Royal Air Force) that had broken the world air speed record in 1953. Mafraq was about a one-and-a-half-hour drive from Amman and few of the pilots had cars to make the journey so I was lucky to have bumped into him when I did.

Muwaffaq told me that many of his friends in England called him 'Frank', perhaps because they had trouble pronouncing his name. He was wonderful company, and very attractive, but I was having too much fun on the Amman social scene to be thinking about a serious relationship with any one man. I was also aware that Jordanian men can be very protective of their women once they are in a relationship, which can feel to an English woman like a rather stifling possessiveness. I didn't feel ready for that and found it unsettling that Muwaffaq was almost immediately showing signs of feeling that way about me. I was still only in my very early twenties and didn't like the idea of having my movements and freedoms restricted by an overprotective boyfriend, however attractive he might be, just as the wider world seemed to be opening up to me.

The fighter pilots cut very glamorous figures in Jordanian society, partly because of their personal attributes, partly because of the daredevil nature of their work and partly because of their favoured position in the King's inner circle of friends and companions. As I started to go out with Muwaffaq more frequently, we often went to parties at the King's home outside Amman, a small, modest house where he and Princess Muna lived much of the time with their two sons, and at another of his houses, in the Jordan Valley, where we would have a great time playing silly games and dancing to Spanish music.

His Majesty loved flying himself, both in planes and helicopters, saying it was the only time he felt totally free. I was in a helicopter with him piloting once and it was obvious that he couldn't have been happier. His love of flying was known to worry his mother, although a

British ambassador wrote that they thought he was much safer in the air than on the ground given his other love, driving fast cars.

The links between the Jordanian and British air forces stretch back a long way. The RAF (then known as the Royal Flying Corps) first flew over the skies of Jordan in 1917 during the Arab Revolt. T. E. Lawrence (as in 'Lawrence of Arabia') wrote about the daring raids these biplanes made against the Turks. Since that time, the RAF has remained closely connected with the area. Winston Churchill realised it would be cheaper to police the British-mandated and ruled areas in the Middle East with the Royal Air Force rather than the army, so there were many air bases dotted around Iraq, Jordan, Palestine and Egypt.

King Abdullah I (King Hussein's grandfather) had wanted Jordan to have its own air force, but the British were unwilling to support the idea. In June 1948, however, the Israelis bombed Amman from the air, making the king even more determined to take control of the skies above his country and in 1950, the Arab Legion Air Force was born. On 19 July 1951, the day before he was assassinated, King Abdullah proudly presented the first Jordanian pilots with their wings, with Prince (later King) Hussein at his side.

Until 1956, the air force commanders had been British, but from then on British pilots and technicians helped only with advice and training and when I arrived in the 1960s, the Royal Air Force had an air adviser attached to the embassy. In April 1964, an adviser to the Pakistan Air Force, Hamid Anwar, came to Jordan and stayed for a year. He created the Hashemite Diamond, a team of nine Hunter planes, practically the whole air force, who would perform aerobatics in the sky. Muwaffaq flew on the right wing. It was so exciting driving out to Mafraq and watching them practice, with just a few aircraft at first, then gradually working up to the whole team. They performed many shows for the King around the country. It was terrifying to watch the man I was beginning to fall in love with roaring through the sky, performing ever more elaborate and dangerous manoeuvres. Knowing they were due to fly over Amman one day, I went up one of the highest jebels to take photographs, but I was shaking so violently from nerves that not one of them came out.

Hamid Anwar was a typical fighter pilot – brash, full of confidence and with a larger-than-life personality. When he was first at the air base in Mafraq, he faced a lot of hostility, but managed to break down the barriers with his unarguable expertise as a fighter pilot. There was nothing like getting behind a pilot in record time during practice combat to prove a point. He had been part of an aircraft aerobatics team with the RAF and was a member of the Pakistan Air Force team that made the first loop with sixteen aircraft. He was more than ready to put the RJAF through its paces.

Anwar's year with the RJAF was an exciting one. He introduced a donkey called Francis to the squadron at Mafraq and the pilot who performed worst each day had to look after him. At first it created quite an upset, as calling an Arab 'a donkey' is a grave insult but soon everyone joined in the spirit of the exercise. It was claimed that the shooting and rocketing scores actually did improve after Francis arrived. The King must have been pleased, because he rewarded Anwar with a bright-red Ford Mustang, one of six that had been given to him by an American oil prospector.

In the early sixties it was much more difficult than it is today to get to some of the more hidden architectural treasures that Jordan had to offer. We usually needed a Land-Rover and a compass to find our way and navigate the terrain, making it feel like more of an adventure than just driving along a well-tarmacked main road. We used to put a picnic together and drive off for the whole day. The British assistant military attache had an ancient Land-Rover in which we would bounce around, getting covered in the mixture of sand and dust that got into everything. Often, we would come across army units on our travels, who would invite us to join them for glasses of tea. They were always so hospitable and I dare say they enjoyed a bit of company to break up their tedious patrolling routines. After providing us with a refreshing drink, they would point us in the right direction for the various castles we wanted to see. Black tea, I discovered, would quench my desert thirst much more satisfactorily than any cold, fizzy drink.

Today, two of the most famous desert castles, Amra and Kharaneh, have a major highway passing within walking distance of them, which makes it convenient for tourists but removes the atmosphere of mystery and antiquity for those of us who remember the way things were. It used to take us hours to find them, now it is a forty-minute drive from the city. Azraq castle, where Emir Faisal and T. E. Lawrence temporarily had their headquarters during the Arab Revolt, was situated in the middle of the most wonderful oasis when I was first introduced to it. Now, it is surrounded by a town, with the main road running along its outer walls. There used to be masses of water in the pools of the oasis and we would swim in them if we could find some privacy. The abundant water also encouraged migrating birds to use Azraq as a stop-over, making the whole area teem with wildlife, but sadly this has now almost disappeared because so much of the water has been pumped out for the drinking and washing needs of the ever-increasing human population. The area is now home to the largest air base in Jordan – the Muwaffaq Salti Air Base.

The British embassy had a small hunting lodge at the oasis, where people could sleep overnight in order to rise early for shooting in the morning. One day I heard that a party was heading there for sport. Hating the thought of so many beautiful birds being shot, I called up Muwaffaq.

'Can you do some low flying in that area tomorrow morning, early?' I asked.

'Sure,' he replied.

The shooting party all came back the following day, swearing at the air force for spoiling their sport. I never confessed.

The embassy also had a small cottage in Jericho with a large, cement-lined hole in the garden which, when filled with water, became a swimming pool, providing enough space for about two strokes one way and three the other. It was so idyllic to be able to go down in the middle of winter and eat outside, picking oranges straight from the trees for dessert.

One lovely spring day, we drove to Qumran, overlooking the Dead Sea, and explored the caves where the Dead Sea Scrolls had been found by a shepherd boy in 1948. I regret that I didn't do more exploring on the West Bank when it was possible, because in 1967, during what came to be known as the 'Six Day War', it was occupied by the Israelis and was no longer accessible to daytrippers from Jordan. That was the start of what would become the longest occupation in modern history, during which Israel has committed major violations of international human rights law, including the practice of collective punishment, building illegal settlements and the killing of innocent people in its administration of the occupied Palestinian territories. It was at this stage, over half a century ago, that I started to understand the politics of the area a little better, which was why I was less surprised by what happened in Gaza in 2023 than many others and why I felt strongly enough to be marching and protesting around London in my eighties.

Everyone who comes to Jordan has to experience a swim in the Dead Sea, although it is not something to enjoy on a regular basis. We used to go down there a lot in the 1960s. There was horse racing and even a casino for a while. The feeling of floating on the salty water with a newspaper held up for a photograph is unique, but great care has to be taken to wash off every speck of salt afterwards, otherwise your skin will itch unbearably. Contrary to popular belief, it *is* possible to drown in the Dead Sea, although your body won't actually sink. There was one incident where more than twenty cadets drowned.

Nowadays, commercialisation and tourism have taken over the region, as with so many other ancient cultures, and the contents of the sea are being used for bath salts, shampoo, mud masks and many other cosmetic and health products. The headwaters from the River Jordan no longer flow like they used to because they are being diverted for other projects along the way and the water levels have consequently dropped dramatically. Hotels that were once situated directly beside the lapping waves have had to build more and more walkways and steps for guests to be able to get down to the water.

It is obvious that the distribution of water in the region is unfair. Anyone can see that the Israeli settlers have green lawns and swimming pools, while the Palestinians have virtually no water. The Israelis have also been known to pour concrete down the Palestinians' wells and cut down their olive trees, all to make the land uninhabitable for them, in order to force them out. It is a process which has been going on, in plain sight, for many years.

We also took trips to Jerusalem, Ramallah and Nablus, driving down to the Rift Valley and crossing the River Jordan, which was not the wide river I imagined it would be. Compared with most of the world's famous rivers, it's more like a stream. Driving up the other side of the valley, we would stop and wander through the little stone villages we came across, most of which had their own mosques and minarets, some with churches, and through the olive groves scattered among the hillsides and fields. It was all so beautiful. It felt like we were bringing biblical stories to life. We could travel easily to all these places in the West Bank, even though there were constant outbreaks of trouble between the Jordanians and the Palestinians, even when the West Bank was still part of Jordan.

From the East Bank of the River Jordan, on a clear day, we could catch glimpses of Jerusalem and driving up to this historical city was always an indescribably uplifting and exciting experience. It is easy to understand why so many have fought for it down the centuries. Strolling in the narrow streets of the Old City felt like walking in the footsteps of the famous biblical figures I had read about in school. The dark and gloomy Church of the Holy Sepulchre didn't have much atmosphere but the Garden Tomb was wonderfully tranquil, if you could find a moment when no one else was there. Standing on the Mount of Olives and looking over Jerusalem literally took my breath away, even though I had no religious beliefs of my own.

Visiting Jerusalem with Muwaffaq was an intensely moving and otherworldly experience for me, although on one occasion he was mistaken for my tourist guide and was banned from entering one of the sites, which severely dented his fighter pilot's pride. On another visit, we were walking in the Old City when a young Jordanian woman approached us with a broad smile. Muwaffaq obviously knew her well and chatted to her for ages without introducing me. I felt a disturbing pang of jealousy and once we had moved on I asked who she was.

'That is my sister, Hanna,' he said. 'She is teaching in a school right on the border with Israel.'

I was relieved to hear that she was a relative and not an ex-girlfriend, but I was still surprised by how jealous I had felt at the sight of him talking to an attractive woman I didn't know. It seemed I cared about him more than I was admitting, even to myself.

5

'Don't Kiss Me Here'

AFTER ONLY SIX MONTHS in Jordan, I realised that I wanted to marry Muwaffaq.

I'm not sure what made me so certain when previously I had been cautious about giving up my independence, but I do know the moment it happened. Towards the end of October, in 1964, I went with some friends from Amman to visit Umm al-Jimal, (an ancient, ruined city built of black basalt, about ten kilometres east of Mafraq), collecting Anwar's American wife from the air base on the way.

Anwar, the Pakistani air force advisor, decided to give us an air show while we were there and flew over the ruins with great panache. It was a breathtaking sight accompanied by the deafening roar of the plane. We returned to his house for dinner and Muwaffaq joined us. It was at that moment, as he strode confidently into the room, that I knew I wanted to spend the rest of my life with him. As he had been courting me so assiduously, I was pretty sure that he felt the same way about me. I wasn't so sure, however, that he would think it appropriate to ask me, since there was already a movement to stop pilots from marrying foreign women and I had not really encouraged him up to that point. He was also aware that he would be asking me to give up a lot in order to live a military life on an air base in the middle of the desert. Being such a proud man, I knew he wouldn't have liked the idea of being rejected and I suspected that this would inhibit him from taking the plunge.

So, a few weeks after that dinner revelation, still feeling convinced it was the right thing to do, I summoned up my courage to break with tradition and I asked him to marry me. To my relief, he accepted without hesitation. The custom was that I then wore a ring on my right hand, to show the world I was spoken for, which Muwaffaq would transfer to my left hand once we were married.

Having only been in the Middle East for six months, I still had a lot to learn about local customs and expectations. The first party I held in my flat, for instance, once Muwaffaq and I had announced that we were a couple, nearly became a social disaster. I had yet to understand the Arab way of entertaining, where guests expect to see the table groaning with food. I had prepared what I thought was an adequate number of dishes, hoping, in my frugal British way, that there wouldn't be anything left over to go to waste. Imagine the horror of my future husband when he arrived, a short while before everyone else, to find such a miserly display of food. He rushed straight back out and bought all sorts of things, managing to make the table look as if it would feed a hundred. Needless to say, I was eating the leftovers for days afterwards, but our honour was preserved in the eyes of our friends and I had learned an important lesson.

On 21 December 1964, RJAF Hunters engaged in the first aerial dog fight with the Mirages of the Israeli Air Force. The battle took place over the West Bank, near the Dead Sea. Muwaffaq wasn't involved, but other friends were and they were euphoric at how well it had gone with no casualties on our side. The next day, the Israeli English-language newspaper had headlines about how Jordanian aircraft had intruded into Israeli air space and had been chased off, but a flight lieutenant from the British Royal Air Force, who was in the Jordanian radar station at the time, told us that he actually saw the Israelis flying into Jordanian air space. I was shocked to discover that the truth could be the complete opposite to what was appearing in the media. The Israelis' propaganda machine, I realised, was much more effective than ours, and still is. I have rarely believed anything I have read or heard in the media since that day.

I didn't inform my family of my engagement immediately because Jill, my middle sister, was due to visit Jordan and I thought it would be a good idea for her to meet Muwaffaq first, so that she could reassure them when she got home that I was marrying a good man. She did a lot of sightseeing while she was with me, actually getting to Petra, Wadi Rum and Aqaba before I did. We have some lovely photos of her in Wadi Rum, surrounded by the splendid-looking soldiers of the Camel Corps. Glubb Pasha first recruited Bedouins from the desert in the 1930s in order to subdue tribal unrest and he personally designed their uniform, consisting of a long khaki robe with white trousers underneath and cross bands of red leather holding ammunition and a pistol. On their heads they wear the traditional Arab headdress, (*keffiyeh*), in chequered red and white with a black *agal* (a head rope which originated from a camel tether). Because of their flowing robes and the curled locks they wore in the 1930s, they were nicknamed 'Glubb's Girls'. The camels looked equally splendid with their colourful woven saddlebags and tassels, living up to their name, 'ships of the desert', wearing the most disdainful air as they plod steadily along. The Camel Corps are still patrolling the desert to deter cross-border smugglers today.

With the typical self-centredness of the young, I brushed aside all thoughts of how shocked and worried my family in England might feel about my marriage announcement when it landed on their doormat out of the blue. I just wanted Muwaffaq and nothing and nobody was going to deter me. The fact that Jill had met and liked him should, it seemed to me, be enough to put their minds at rest. Many years later, my mother showed me the letter I wrote to them, informing them that

I was going to marry a Jordanian who they knew nothing about and I blushed when I read it. My family had never even met an Arab and in the 1960s it must have been quite a shock to receive such unexpected news when their daughter had only been away for a matter of months. I didn't have much tact then, and my friends would probably say I haven't changed much in the intervening years. Despite the abrupt announcement, my parents were very understanding and as supportive as ever. The only opinion my father proffered was, 'it's not going to be a bed of roses, you know,' which was a pretty succinct, and accurate, prediction of what was to come. One of my aunts was a little more proactive and actually wrote to the Foreign Office, telling them off for allowing me to marry an Arab and she was by no means the only one in the family who was unhappy about it. There were other relations and friends who couldn't believe that my parents could allow me to marry a Muslim, notwithstanding the fact that they (my parents, that is) didn't have any choice in the matter, since I was over twenty-one and had a mind of my own. It wouldn't have mattered what any of them had said or done, I would still have gone ahead.

I guess there was still a stereotype in British people's minds then that Arabs were all cheats and liars, which was really just a matter of different cultures not understanding the subtleties of one another's traditions and customs. I used to play cards with Muwaffaq, for instance, and I kept winning when I knew he was a much better player.

'Why aren't you winning?' I demanded. 'You must be cheating!'

'I know,' he said. 'I wanted you to win.'

'But cheating isn't part of the game,' I protested.

'Why not?' he asked, genuinely puzzled, since to him it most definitely was all part of the game.

Muwaffaq never asked me to become a Muslim; he left the choice entirely up to me. Since I have always been totally irreligious, having been put off the whole idea during my convent schooldays, I never even thought about it. Not that I didn't enjoy sitting on the edge of the Citadel at the top of Jabal al-Qalaa, the highest of Amman's seven hills, on a fine evening, gazing down at the panorama of the city below and listening to the haunting echoes of the muezzin calling the faithful to prayer or walking around the streets of Jerusalem, soaking up the atmosphere created by so many centuries of different faiths and beliefs. As a gesture to my future husband and his family, I did start to learn Arabic, but I am ashamed to say that many years later I am still absolutely hopeless at it and, since almost everyone I met spoke English, I was able to get away with it.

Muwaffaq was the leading light of his family, being the first-born boy, and, as far as I can remember, the only objection to our marriage on his side came from his second brother, who couldn't believe that his beloved elder sibling could possibly marry a foreign woman. Sixty years later, however, he is now with his second English wife and living in the UK.

I dare say that despite the family's kindness towards me there were probably some resentments simmering in the background, but I knew nothing about them at the time. One of my sisters-in-law said to me later: 'The problem is that you foreign women took all our best men.'

'I'm sorry,' I replied, 'but all your best men took us. Why do you suppose that was?'

However accepting our families might have been, the British embassy wouldn't countenance the idea of having a member of staff engaged to a Jordanian, seeing it as a security risk, although they had no problem with us continuing with an affair, which was what many others did. They told me I had to choose between my job and Muwaffaq. So, I chose Muwaffaq. I sold my car, paid back the rest of the loan to the Foreign Office and flew back to England to take some time off with my family in order to be sure that I wanted to go ahead with such a major life decision. I spent the whole flight in floods of tears at the thought of being away from him, even for a short time. In my heart I was already quite certain I was doing the right thing.

I found the transition from life in Amman back to life in Wolverhampton shockingly hard to cope with, particularly as there was no proper telephone link with Jordan, only wireless, and letters took weeks to arrive. Although it was lovely to see my family again, my memory of those four months in England is a complete haze because all I could think of was getting back to Jordan and back to Muwaffaq.

Then I received the wonderful news that he was coming to England with Jihad, another pilot, ferrying two Hunters over for refurbishing. It was the perfect opportunity for him to meet my family. Just as I expected, the months without him had not made any difference to my feelings, if anything they had intensified them and the sight of him walking towards me at RAF Lyneham overwhelmed me. I ran to greet him with my arms outstretched.

'Don't kiss me now!' he hissed.

This was another lesson to be learned. In the Arab world, public displays of affection are frowned upon and this rule extended to England whenever Muwaffaq was in the company of fellow Jordanians.

My mother had lent me her car for the reunion, so when Muwaffaq and Jihad then flew from Lyneham to Dunsfold, a flight lasting about ten minutes, I had to drive there and the journey seemed to take hours.

A big family party was organised in South London, so poor Muwaffaq was thrown straight in at the deep end, meeting my parents, sisters and various aunts, uncles and cousins, all in one go. It never occurred to me that it was a strange, or even brave, thing for an English woman to marry an Arab. He was just the person I loved. So, when we were out shopping together in Wolverhampton, I was genuinely puzzled at the looks we were getting until I realised that people were staring at us because I was white and he was so very dark and they had never seen a couple like us before. It was a revelation to me to discover that complete strangers might find that remarkable.

Unfortunately, Muwaffaq's holiday was cut short as he was ordered back to Amman to fly in the Hashemite Diamond for President Ayub Khan of Pakistan. By the time he got back to Jordan the presidential visit had been cancelled, so he could have stayed in England longer but at least, I thought, my family had had a chance to meet him and, hopefully, felt reassured that he loved me and would look after me.

After four months in England, even more certain now that I was doing the right thing, I packed my bags once more, brimming with anticipation and excitement, and set off for Jordan for the second time, this time by air.

When Muwaffaq met me at Amman Airport, surrounded by many of his friends, he was dressed very smartly. Only later did I discover that they weren't actually his own clothes – he had come from Mafraq in his uniform and one of his friends had said he couldn't possibly meet his future wife dressed like that, then proceeded to lend him his clothes.

'Don't kiss me here!' he reminded me.

6

Extended Family

ON 14 JULY 1965, Muwaffaq and I were married. I dare say Muwaffaq's family would have liked a full-scale celebration with me in a traditional white dress sitting in the corner of the room and everyone celebrating around me. In reality, it was a mad dash to a sheikh's house with me in a summer dress and two friends, Isam, a helicopter pilot, and Awni, a transport pilot, both of whom, much to my irritation, kept telling Muwaffaq that he still had time to change his mind. Fortunately, he took no notice of them.

In Arab countries it is customary when a marriage is arranged, for the families to negotiate what the future husband will be able to provide for his prospective bride. We had no such framework to work with since his family had no money and he was surviving on his meagre air force salary. We had, however, drawn up an agreement as to what the financial situation would be if we were to divorce. As far as I remember, all I asked for was that I would receive enough for a British Airways airfare back to England. Like most young people in love, I really didn't give my financial future any thought at all.

The sheikh had a towel wrapped around his head – maybe we had got him out of the shower – and his son was still wandering around in his pyjamas. I didn't understand a single word of the whole rite, but signed my wedding certificate with complete confidence that everything was going to be all right. Muwaffaq and I then left in a taxi to go to his family home as a married couple.

'Muwaffaq,' I said, holding out my hands as we sat together in the backseat, 'do you think you could put the ring on my wedding finger now?'

It was certainly not a romantic affair, but it didn't matter a whit to me because I had never dreamed of, or even wanted, a traditional white wedding. All that mattered was that this kind, brave, handsome man was now my husband and we would be together for the rest of our lives. We were the last couple to marry before a ban, forbidding members of the military to marry foreigners, came in, which seemed like another sign that our union was meant to be. I was very happy.

We started our honeymoon in his family home, which was not ideal, considering you could hear every word and every movement through the walls of every room. One of my biggest problems on all of our visits to the family home was coping with this lack of privacy.

There were about thirty steps to get down to the house, which was built into the side of a hill. It consisted of two bedrooms, a kitchen and a bathroom at the back, with no windows, and in the middle were two rooms which were the dining room and the family room. On the outside was another bedroom and the formal salon where guests were entertained.

The Arabic-style toilet was sunk into the floor, with a tap and a plastic jug in place of a flush and toilet paper. For someone who liked her privacy and time in the loo, this was pure torture. Everyone saw you enter and if you had constipation, heaven help your leg muscles, followed by the embarrassment of everyone seeing when you staggered out after ten minutes. It was difficult to manage without toilet paper, and if I wanted to have a shower, the water had to be heated on the cooker in a large pan. The pan was then taken into the bathroom, where I sat on a stool and used a can to scoop up the water and throw it over myself. It is amazing what you can deal with when you are in love, although I have to admit that once I got more confident, I would ask Muwaffaq to take me up to the InterContinental to use their facilities.

It is hard to make love when you think that the whole family can hear every movement, although I suppose it did generate some element of the forbidden, which made it quite exciting. At least for us it was only for short visits and then we could go back to the privacy of our own home. How married couples who live with extended family carry on an intimate relationship when the whole family live so close, I cannot imagine. I suppose the answer is that they don't, and maybe they wouldn't even want to, and that is how their lives are anyway.

After a few days we went to our new home to begin our married life, on the air base at Mafraq, in the middle of the desert. There were three other English girls there: Margaret, who was married to an engineer, and Clare and Janet, whose husbands were fighter pilots, like Muwaffaq. We didn't have an assigned house at first, so I stayed with Clare and her husband, Ihsan. She and I slept together on the hardest bed I have ever slept on, before or since. Ihsan slept downstairs on the settee and Muwaffaq slept in the mess. Why I didn't sleep on the settee I don't know.

The air base at Mafraq was established by the British in the 1930s and had expanded over the years, before being handed over to the Jordanians in 1957. It was situated in the middle of nowhere, about eighty kilometres from Amman, with nothing but sand and dust blowing in all directions. There was a small village about five kilometres away, now a large town with a famous tuberculosis hospital, Annoor Sanatorium, which was originally set up to help the bedouin. It was run for many years by an intrepid American lady. The highway that went past the base was the main road to Iraq. As you approached from the village, you could see the trees that had been planted over the years with simple houses scattered among them, built when the RAF was stationed there in the 1940s and 1950s. Inside the main entrance were the villas for the senior officers, then the semi-detached houses for junior officers, all constructed of local stone and with flat roofs. There were trenches in front of the houses in case we were attacked, although I don't think anyone could have persuaded me to jump into them. I was much too frightened of the scorpions and snakes that I was convinced were lying in wait for me.

I didn't enjoy the housework, nor the cooking, but luckily Muwaffaq did enjoy cooking (though not the washing up), so we didn't starve. Shopping lists had to be compiled for a driver who went into Mafraq village in the mornings. The choice was basic – fruit, vegetables and meat. Chickens had to be gutted, which proved a pitfall to unwary young foreign wives. Margaret told me that the first time she proudly dished up roast chicken to her new husband when he got home from work there was a suspiciously bad smell lingering in the air. He asked if she had taken the insides out, which of course she had not. So, over the wall went the chicken for the dogs to feast on and a lesson was learned.

In one early attempt at domesticity, I tried dishing up a cauliflower cheese, but inadvertently made it with sweet condensed milk. Muwaffaq valiantly swallowed a mouthful and tried to assure his new bride that it was delicious. As soon as I had a taste, however, it went straight into the rubbish bin. How lovely new husbands are, at least mine was.

Laundry had to be done by hand, which meant washing the sheets in the bath. I would then stagger down the stairs with sheets that weighed a ton because I couldn't wring much of the water out of them. Throwing them over the clothesline was even more difficult, as I struggled not to let the ends touch the dusty ground. In the summer there were also flies to contend with, landing on my face and clinging on tenaciously while I frantically tried to peg out the heavy, water-logged sheets.

Cockroaches were my greatest enemy. I couldn't bear to put my foot on them because of the awful crunching noise, so I used spray – masses of it – nearly asphyxiating myself in the process. One morning a huge cockroach was perched on the stairs, so I was trapped upstairs with no spray until Muwaffaq came home for lunch. On another occasion I was out in the garden and an enormous locust landed on the flyscreen at the back door. I couldn't get rid of it and couldn't bring myself to open the door. However much I hated all these creatures, I really didn't like to kill them either.

Many aspects of life on the base were still quite primitive. A visit to the dentist, for instance, took a lot of nerve as the drill was driven by a foot pump, but the cinema was fun and occasionally they would show old western films, which drew an enthusiastic audience. Sometimes we would be mystified by the apparent illogicality of a film, until it dawned on us that the reels had been put on in the wrong order. Going to the cinema outside the base was also an experience, with chairs so hard I would have to take a cushion with me. Everyone ate dried melon seeds, which came in various forms – roasted, baked, salted, etc. They were put into the mouth one at a time and with great manipulation the shells were cracked open with the teeth and spat out onto the floor. The tiny seed that was left was duly chewed and swallowed, although to me it hardly seemed worth the effort. Most Jordanians, however, are very adept at this ritual and by the end of the film we would have to crunch our way out over the empty shells. The practice has now been banned.

So, our domestic life went on through that hot summer, enduring the sandstorms that would force their way through every crack and keyhole, leaving us half suffocated and the house covered in a thick layer of sand. If you cleaned it away, an hour later it was back again.

My parents had given us £180 for our wedding present, which we spent on a cooker and a refrigerator. We bought bamboo furniture for our sitting room and the dining room and bedroom furniture we bought from a carpenter in monthly payments. A second-hand carpet for the sitting-room floor came from downtown. Muwaffaq loved entertaining and was always inviting people over to eat. He did most of the cooking in secret. I'm not sure whether it was because he didn't want to admit to doing it and risk tarnishing his manly image or whether he didn't want to admit that he had married a woman who couldn't even manage an edible cauliflower cheese.

We didn't get back to visit Muwaffaq's family in Amman much, but we were sometimes given a lift by a friend who had a car (it took about an hour and a half) or, more often, we took a series of three taxis, one from Amman to Zerqa, then Zerqa to Mafraq village and finally, to the base. These taxis would be the service ones, which carried two passengers in the front and three in the back. They had no air conditioning and the radio would always be blaring loud Arabic music, with everyone puffing away on cigarettes as we swerved around oncoming cars and lorries.

There always seemed to be hundreds of visiting relatives in the family house in Amman, all shouting at the same time, seeming to be furious about whatever subject they were discussing, but they were wonderfully kind to me, this strange, foreign person their son had thrust into their midst.

Both his parents were illiterate, but Umm Muwaffaq was determined her children would succeed in the modern world, which meant they had to have an education. She ruled the home and her simple and devout faith in God carried her through all the pains in her life. Apart from Muwaffaq and his eldest sister, Nawal, all her children went to university, thanks to her determination.

When I first knew her, a black scarf covered her face completely, then in later years, a white one covered her hair. Originally from Syria, my mother-in-law was a wonderful cook who loved plants, which she had massed on the veranda, where the family would meet and talk amidst bougainvillea, jasmine, vines and hydrangeas, all intermingling their blossoms and their scents, all planted in colourful used tins. The flower-covered veranda was where we all sat together and talked on warm evenings, overlooking the wadi.

Her ability to feed seven or more offspring as well as any visitors who might drop in filled me with admiration. Cooking would be a community affair, with relatives or friends sitting and chatting while stuffing vine leaves, marrows, aubergines and any other vegetable that was appropriate, washing and sorting mounds of spinach, cleaning and soaking rice, or any of the other preparations needed. At the end of the day, they all went home with their share, having had a great day of gossiping. I loved the food, apart from the yoghurt that is used in much of the cooking, although I still liked to eat English food when I could.

My father-in-law, Abu Muwaffaq, was a bandsman in the Arab Legion in his early days, going on to build houses for a living. He was generous to a fault, giving money away to anyone who came to him with a hard-luck story, sometimes forgetting about the needs of his own family in the process. Despite causing them a lot of pain, he was much loved by them all. He lived to the fine old age of ninety-two, when he was knocked over by a taxi and killed. Even though he smoked like a chimney all his life, he walked everywhere. When he was in his eighties, my brother-in-law felt guilty about this and decided to devote a whole day to ferrying his father around in the car. It took them just a couple of hours to finish all the daily chores. He then realised he hadn't done his father a favour after all and it would be better to leave him to carry on as usual, since that meant his whole day would be filled and he would get plenty of exercise at the same time.

On our weekends in Amman, we would go shopping downtown, which was fun for me, but could sometimes be a difficult exercise in restraint for Muwaffaq. The shops were all in a maze of narrow, shaded streets, full of people bustling among the displays. Policemen in Germanic spiked helmets would be directing the traffic, which was a great challenge, and still is, since everyone invented their own rules and zebra crossings were completely ignored by drivers. Eventually, the authorities introduced traffic lights, but still no one seemed to know what they were supposed to do with them.

Muwaffaq had cousins who owned shops amidst this melee, selling dresses and materials, which we would visit. Being a foreigner always attracted attention on the street, and not always of the nicest kind. I quickly learned to keep my eyes on the ground and close my ears to the words some men shouted at me, accusing me of being a 'Western prostitute'. Other foreign women I met found it more difficult to ignore the insults and felt quite threatened. One day we were strolling along, looking at all the goods on display, when Muwaffaq suddenly pushed me through a shop door and ordered me to stay there. A few minutes later, he came in and told me to walk back home and he would follow shortly. I did as he said and half an hour later, he arrived back with a scratch and bruise on his face. When I asked what had happened, he explained that a man had made a comment to me and he had had a fight with him.

'What did the man say?' I asked, imagining it must have been something horrendous.

'He said "hallo".'

I was quite upset, thinking this was a harmless offence and, at the same time, I thanked the heavens the man hadn't said anything worse.

In Mafraq village it was even more difficult to walk about, as foreigners were seen as complete aliens due to our rarity. Whenever I ventured into the village, the car would be surrounded within minutes by a crowd of children, unabashedly peering through the windows to get a glimpse of this strange, pale foreign specimen.

The month of Ramadan was always an interesting time. Devout Muslims would refrain from food, drink and sex between the hours of sunrise and sunset. Restaurants were closed (apart from those in hotels) and there were very strict rules to follow, including no eating, drinking or smoking in public. Being a non-smoker, I enjoyed the smoke-free atmosphere during the day, but hated everyone lighting up at sunset. I didn't fast, but was always careful not to eat or drink in front of those who did.

After a day of fasting, families then meet up just before sunset and join together for a meal. When Ramadan falls during the summer (it follows a lunar calendar and each year it starts ten days earlier) people go out and stroll, meet in cafes, look at the shops and then go to bed very late. Working hours are shorter and an air of lethargy permeates life during this month. Tempers become frayed and the standards of driving get even worse than usual.

When I first arrived in the family, I was shocked at how the men ruled over everything and how the girls were seen as being there just to serve them. If, for instance, my brother-in-law came in late at night when everyone was in bed, he would call for one of his sisters to get up from her bed to fetch him a glass of water. I was always inciting the women to mutiny, but never got very far. Even now, when their brothers visit them, my sisters-in-law will still rush to do their bidding.

Muwaffaq would never order me to do anything, but he knew exactly how to get me to agree to whatever he wanted, having discovered that if it were a logical request, I would concur. He would never say 'don't do this' or 'don't do that' because he knew that would be like a red flag to a bull.

'Trish,' he would say, 'I would rather you didn't go swimming, as it isn't nice for me, as your husband, to have other men I know looking at you.'

I could see his reasoning and I was the new arrival in his world, so I didn't go swimming if there were men around. I also gave up horse-back riding, though this was mainly because I couldn't easily get to the nearest stables, which were at the army camp in Zerqa. By both being polite and reasonable, we managed not to argue much about anything.

Those first few months of marriage were the happiest in my life. Muwaffaq flew to England again with a senior pilot, Nasri, but this time I stayed in Amman. When they were due back, I went to Mafraq with Nasri's wife Randa and their son Samer to meet them, only to find their flight had been delayed and we didn't know where they were. In fact, they were stuck at El Adem in Libya, which was then an RAF base, due to a technical fault on Muwaffaq's aircraft. When this was eventually fixed, they carried on to Cyprus. We then got a call to say they had left Cyprus and would be at Mafraq very soon. Randa and I rushed out and stood gazing up at the sky. Finally, our husbands arrived, flying close to each other over the base, before dramatically peeling off and landing. A few minutes later, the Land-Rover arrived and they jumped out. Yet again I heard the warning, 'Don't kiss me now.'

In early 1966, Muwaffaq was sent on a course to RAF Chivenor in the UK, to become a pilot attack instructor. I went with him and took the opportunity to stay with my parents in Wolverhampton. For the next four months he would come up for some weekends (which meant spending six hours on the train each way) and I would suffer the same inhibitions as I did in Jordan. Making love in the family home, even if it was with my own husband, embarrassed me to such an extent that we would often have frustrated weekends.

Again, I found out how different it was to be married to an Arab. We were at a party at RAF Chivenor one night and everyone was dancing except Muwaffaq and myself. I couldn't understand why no one else had asked me to dance until my husband confessed that he had warned all the men that if they danced with me, he would put a knife in their back. Strangely, his possessiveness didn't worry me, perhaps because it was never overt and only showed itself in English company.

Despite the obstacles to romance in my family home, when we returned to Jordan, I discovered I was pregnant. It was lovely to be back in the privacy of our own home, but soon I began to feel terribly ill. The heat, coupled with pregnancy, made every day an ordeal. I would get up with Muwaffaq in the mornings and stagger downstairs, prepared to do so much with my morning, but when he got home at lunchtime I would still be lying on the settee where he had left me, unable to move. A check-up in the army hospital in Amman revealed that I had hepatitis and although I returned home to Mafraq, life soon became so impossible that I was eventually taken back to Amman and admitted to hospital, where I stayed for a very miserable fortnight.

It is strange what you worry about when you are lying in a hospital bed with nothing to distract you. The hairs on my legs were growing apace and, having no razor with me, I asked one of the nurses if she could possibly get me one. I couldn't wait another minute. You would have thought I had asked for the impossible, which maybe it was as Arab girls mostly waxed their legs. Finally, she brought me an incredible thing that seemed to be missing some important pieces, but did at least have a very blunt blade. I spent an awkward half-hour scraping off those horrid hairs, which boosted my morale a little. My sisters-in-law had once tried to wax my legs with the mixture of sugar and water they used themselves, but it was such a painful experience I decided to stick with the razor.

Being a voracious reader, and having nothing else to do with the endless hours in bed, I read the extraordinary range of books that Muwaffaq managed to find for me. From *And Quiet Flows the Don* to *The Life of Michelangelo*, from a history of the First World War to a variety of light romances, I devoured them all. Strangely, I never seemed to read any political books or any histories of the Middle East and I remained mostly ignorant of what was going on around me. At that time, it was difficult to make comments about anything political for fear of offending the wrong people. In fact, before we were married, Muwaffaq had been court-martialled after he and a colleague, while swimming in a pool, had not stood to attention when the national anthem was played. They hadn't even heard the music. We didn't criticise, or even discuss what the government was doing or the direction the country was going. We lived in the cocooned little world of Mafraq, following orders and getting on with the routines of our daily lives. I would spend many happy hours helping Muwaffaq prepare his lectures, since aviation and the military have always held a fascination for me.

Being discharged from hospital after two weeks was a huge relief and hoping not to see the place again until I was ready to give birth, I went off with great optimism to my in-laws so that they could look after me for a few days before I returned home to Mafraq. The following morning, however, I woke up with stomach pains. They gradually worsened and by lunchtime it was decided to take me back to the hospital I had so happily left the day before. This time, the doctors were worried about all sorts of things. Late that evening they operated and found that I had acute appendicitis. I woke up in the intensive care ward to see Muwaffaq standing beside the bed, looking concerned.

'Is the baby all right?' I asked.

'Yes,' he assured me, so I fell straight back to sleep.

I was transferred from the ICU back to the ward on a trolley, along the internal hospital road, and then taken on a stretcher up the stairs at an angle so acute I was sure I was going to slide off. The next few days were spent in an agony of forcing myself to get out of bed and stand upright. The problem was that my stomach was expanding and the rather large scar just didn't have time to mend into a nice, neat line. Finally, I insisted on returning to Mafraq. I was desperate to be back with Muwaffaq. It was almost as if I knew that we didn't have much time left to us.

7
Red Leader is Missing

I WAS AWARE THAT I was married to a man whose chosen profession meant that he was always living on the edge, but perhaps that danger added to the attraction and young people have a tendency to believe they are immortal anyway.

I remember receiving bad news, a two-seater Hunter had crashed and the pilots were killed. Both were unmarried. It was a shock, but it didn't really occur to me that the same thing might happen to Muwaffaq. We were having too much fun and were too excited about becoming parents to be overly bothered by the prospect of our own vulnerability.

The Red Arrows (the British Royal Air Force aerobatics team) came to visit Jordan and we went to Amman to watch their fantastic display. As we drove back to Mafraq that day, two of our pilots buzzed us on the road. What fun flying was for the pilots then, without all the rules and restrictions there are today.

Once, one of the pilots got carried away and flew in a Hunter over a small town outside Amman, where his girlfriend lived. In his desire to impress her and her family, he forgot that on the next hill stood the King's home. The anti-aircraft guns set up to protect His Majesty apparently fired thousands of rounds at him, but luckily, they all missed and he was totally oblivious to the fact that he was being fired upon. I think he got his flying pay stopped for a couple of months for that little stunt, so I hope he impressed the family. We all enjoyed hearing these tales of derring-do.

I don't believe in premonitions, but Muwaffaq and I had a very painful conversation in early November of that year. For some reason that I couldn't fathom, he wanted to discuss what I should do if he were killed. He kept saying that I should marry again if anything happened to him. Although I tried to evade the whole subject, he was absolutely insistent that I should make him this promise. To say I was upset by his insistence would be putting it mildly. I didn't want to sit there, five months pregnant, and have my husband try to make me promise that I would marry again if he died. It was, to me, a fruitless argument. What was the point? And why make such an issue of it? In the end I had to acquiesce just to shut him up, but I have never kept that promise.

I was still quite weak after the hepatitis and the appendix operation, and so thin that even in the sixth month of pregnancy I had only just started to wear maternity clothes.

The morning of 13 November dawned and Muwaffaq got up as usual, put on his flying overalls and bent over the bed to kiss me goodbye.

'I love you,' I murmured, still half asleep.

'I love you too,' he replied and then strode out of the house to go to work.

I will forever be grateful that we exchanged those few words that morning.

•

As I lay there, dozing, I heard the wailing of sirens and through the window I saw aircraft taking off. I assumed it was a practice scramble. Slowly, my morning started. I eventually got dressed and walked down to my friend Margaret's house for a chat and a cup of tea. Then the phone rang and it was one of the other wives asking to speak to me.

'Have you spoken to Muwaffaq?' she asked.

'No, why?'

'Something has happened. I think you should call the squadron and check on him.'

She had already checked on her own husband and spoken to him, so knew he was safe.

I felt ice entering my bloodstream, but forced myself to remain calm. I left Margaret's house. As I walked down the road towards home a Land-Rover sped past, carrying some of the pilots. I smiled at them as if everything was fine and continued on my way. By the time I came into the house, my whole body felt in turmoil. My hands shaking, finding it hard to keep my voice steady, I called the squadron and asked to speak to Muwaffaq. Jasser, one of the pilots, was the one who had to talk to me and he told me that Muwaffaq was giving a lecture. I didn't believe him, but I didn't argue. I don't know how or why, but I just knew Muwaffaq was not with me anymore and that there was nothing I could do about it now. I wasn't thinking that he was dead, just somehow gone. All my emotions had frozen. I was simply waiting for something to happen, for someone to tell me what to do next.

The one o'clock English news from Israel talked of 'an engagement' between the Israeli and Jordanian air forces.

Shortly afterwards, Margaret came down to me. She walked in and lit a cigarette, as if playing for time before having to speak. 'Muwaffaq is missing,' she told me. 'They're looking for him.'

Poor girl to have to be the bearer of such terrible news. I felt I was in the middle of a bad dream – how could he have left me that morning with so much love and now be gone forever? I tried to force myself to focus, to wake up and make the nightmare end. Some of the pilots then came around to tell me that they had found Muwaffaq's body near the Dead Sea. He had ejected, they told me, but was too low for his parachute to deploy. They all swore they would avenge him, but no amount of revenge or angry talk was ever going to help me surface from the tidal wave of misery that swept over me.

In a trance, I did everything they told me to do. I went upstairs to pack a bag and was driven to Amman with Margaret, her husband Michel and a doctor. We arrived at Muwaffaq's family home, where a crowd had already gathered and was continuing to swell. Every one of those thirty steps down the hillside was torture. Halfway down, Isam, one of Muwaffaq's best friends and one of the witnesses at our wedding, was standing, waiting and I just fell into his arms – poor man, it must have embarrassed him dreadfully. Slowly, he helped me through the door, to be confronted by the most terrible scenes of grief, with my mother-in-law wailing and tearing her hair out in clumps. The doctor tried to help, but there was little he could do. I couldn't stay there and was helped up to another relation's house. I was told that Muwaffaq's body was at the military hospital and I insisted on being taken there. I couldn't bear the thought that I would never see his face again. How did I breathe? How did I put one foot in front of the other? Where were my tears? What was happening to me? Nothing made sense. Nothing was clear. At that moment, continuing to live didn't seem possible.

When we arrived at the hospital the English matron took me by the hand and walked me towards the room where they had laid him out. On the left-hand side, on the floor, was his parachute, covered in his blood. On the table was the body of my beloved husband, covered by a sheet up to his handsome face, which was undamaged. I was so nervous. I didn't know what to do. The matron guided me forwards, lifted my hand and placed it gently on his forehead.

'You can touch him, you know,' she said.

All I could say was his name, over and over. I had never seen a dead body before. I couldn't believe that the young man who had been so full of life and love when he left the bedroom that morning was gone.

The physical pain was unbelievable. I was certain my heart was going to break.

Well-meaning, guiding hands took me back to the relation's house and gave me a sleeping pill. When I awoke the next morning there was only one person left in the house and she had no idea what was going on or why I was there. I got dressed. Was this still me? What was happening? Did I have the strength to keep going? I stumbled out into the street and got a taxi back down to the family home.

In Arab countries funerals happen very quickly because of the heat. By the time I arrived at the house everyone was waiting for the coffin, which was to be paraded through the streets before being buried in the royal cemetery. Women don't usually attend funerals, but an air force officer put me in a Land-Rover and I was driven up to the cemetery, where I watched the military rites, with the firing of the guns as the coffin was lowered into the grave by his friends and colleagues. Surely, I told myself, I was going to wake up from this nightmare soon.

One of the King's cousins, Sharif Ghazi Rakan, who was also a fighter pilot, came over to me.

'His Majesty would like you to come and stay with him and Princess Muna at their home in Hommer,' he said. 'It is the King's birthday. He is having a family party.'

I had no idea how I would cope with a party, but I was still happy to accept, not wanting to go back to Mafraq alone or to be in the grief-filled family home. The previous day, President Ayub Khan of Pakistan had arrived on a state visit. So, what with that visit and the aftermath of the battle with the Israelis, the King was exceptionally busy but he and Princess Muna still managed to find time to comfort me and offer me a distraction from the grief that was overwhelming me. It was the first of many, many kindnesses that he would show me over the following years.

Gradually, I was piecing together what had happened to cause my life to take such a terrible turn. The Palestinian *fedayeen* had been making raids into Israel all through the spring and summer of 1966, both from the Syrian and Jordanian borders. On 13 November, the Israelis moved over the border and the attack on the village of Samu began at 5.30 a.m., where, according to the UN report, they destroyed 125 houses, including two shops, a medical clinic, a six-classroom school, a dwelling tent, seventeen military jeeps and a civilian bus. They also damaged a further twenty-three houses and a mosque and killed eight monkeys, four cows and one goat and wounded a camel. At Rum al-Madfa they almost totally destroyed a police post building and left four dead horses. In the village of Jinba they destroyed fifteen stone huts and damaged seven more, killed a camel and destroyed a well.

In Rafat three Jordanian army tents were destroyed by fire and three Jordanian army vehicles were completely obliterated by aerial bombing.

It was a list of destruction that typified the way the Israelis chose to use collective punishment, as would be seen on an even more terrible scale in 2023 when they attacked Gaza with the apparent intention of total destruction.

Muwaffaq and his fellow pilots scrambled to intervene. Muwaffaq and Ihsan (who later became the commander of the Royal Jordanian Air Force) took off, followed by another pair of pilots. As soon as they arrived, however, they were set upon by several Israeli Mirages. Muwaffaq was caught by an Israeli Mirage pilot as he climbed over the hills towards the Dead Sea on his way home. He was the only one not to return.

At 9.30 a.m., the Israelis departed back across the border. Their punitive operation lasted four hours, leaving twenty-one dead and thirty-seven wounded.

The affair was brought before the United Nations, and the Security Council condemned Israel by a large majority. The US Representative, Arthur Goldberg, described the Israeli raid as 'inexcusable'.

After the attack against Samu, things got worse, not only between Jordan and Israel but also between Jordan and her Arab allies, except for Saudi Arabia. From then on, His Majesty became the target of the Syrians, the Egyptians and especially the Palestine Liberation Organization.

Muwaffaq was the first and only Jordanian pilot to be shot down in the air and killed. I have now read about the incident in a variety of history books where the events and surrounding political manoeuvring are all set out in a factual, black-and-white way. At the time, however, like much of what happens in warfare it was all confusion bordering on farce.

It was all so bewildering, the many faces and conversations at the King's party going past me in a blur. When I woke the next morning, I found I had laryngitis and could hardly speak, which was probably a reaction to all the emotional stress. My parents had read about the incident in the newspapers in England, but had told themselves that it couldn't possibly be Muwaffaq so when I phoned to tell them the bad news, they too were shocked and immediately realised that I needed support. My brother-in-law was working and studying in Wolverhampton at the time, so he and my mother immediately booked to fly out to Jordan to be with me.

The King and Princess Muna insisted that I stayed with them until my mother arrived and then she and I moved into the guest palace. I had to go back to Mafraq to pack my things up, which was incredibly painful since everything in the house reminded me of Muwaffaq and all the plans and dreams that we had been building for our future together, with our child.

We decided that I should go back to England to have the baby, which was another shock for my poor Jordanian in-laws. I saw them a few times before we left, but my own shock was too deep for me to be able to offer them any help or comfort. None of us knew what to do or what to say to one another.

When my mother and I arrived at the airport, to catch a BOAC VC10 to London, the flight was held up while everyone waited for the King and Princess Muna to come and say goodbye. They eventually swept onto the tarmac and the King presented me with Muwaffaq's medal for bravery – the Order of Military Gallantry, equivalent to the Victoria Cross in the UK. The other passengers must have wondered what was going on.

As we finally took off, leaving Jordan and my husband's grave behind, I felt I was being torn in half, between two homes and two families.

My husband

Order of Military Gallantry awarded posthumously

My father-in-law

My mother-in-law with her grandson

My mother and father on their wedding day

My mother with her three young daughters

On my way! 1964

My future husband in my parents' garden

My husband outside the house we lived in on the air base in Mafraq

The funeral on 14 November 1966

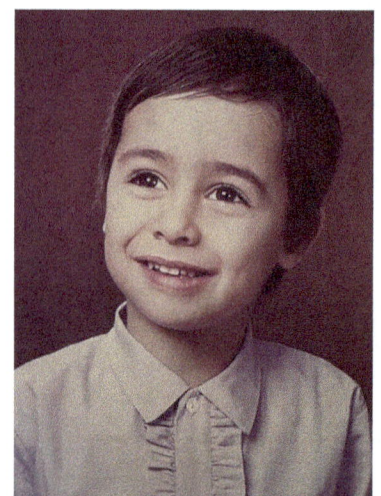 

My lovely son

My father with his grandson

His Majesty King Hussein in work mode in the 1960s

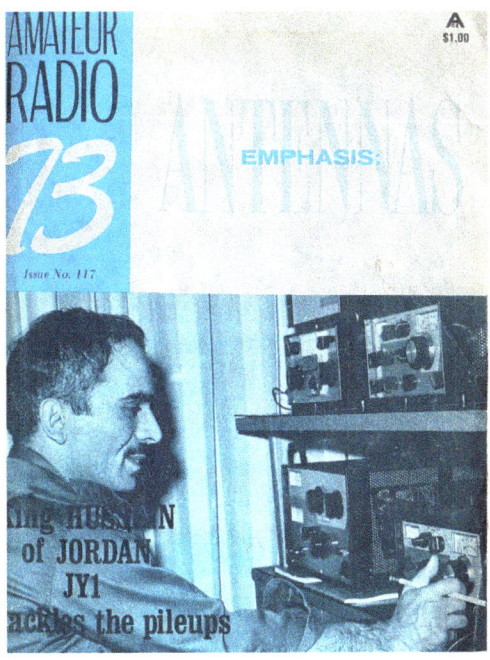

His Majesty on his amateur radio

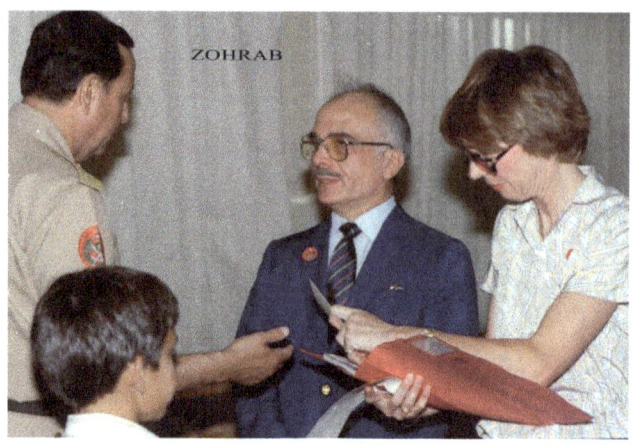

With His Majesty before the Jordan Armed Forces performances at the Royal Tournament, 1985 (photo by Zohrab)

With Her Majesty Queen Noor and Mrs Shaker looking at the photos to go in the Jordanian stand at Earls Court (photo by Zohrab)

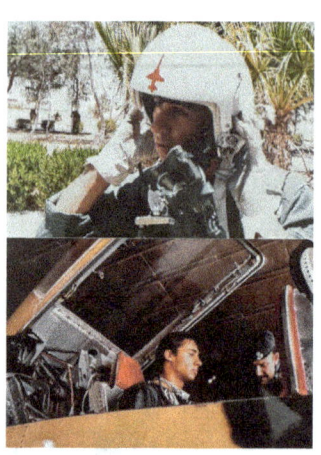

My son having flights in a T37 and an F5

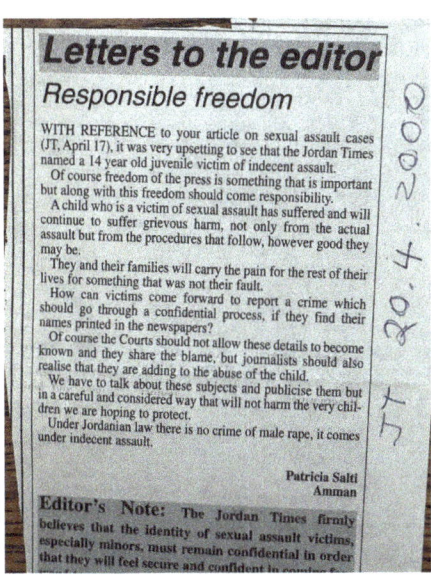

One of many letters I wrote

Receiving my OBE from the then Prince of Wales

With Muwaffaq at Buckingham Palace

Celebrating my OBE

In Bali with Maia and Kiri

My mother on her 90th birthday with my sisters

Family

Having fun in Japan

With Muwaffaq and Angel

Kiri and Maia

Maia and Kiri

With pals on the march for Palestine

On the march, 2024

My wonderful pals in Jordan

Selling melons on the side of the road

Aerial photo of the citadel with the Roman theatre in downtown Amman (photo by Bob Bewley)

The beautiful Wadi Rum (photo by Jane Taylor)

At my husband's grave in the royal cemetery, 2024

8

Returning with Baby Muwaffaq

As our flight approached the UK, the weather closed in and our pilot circled Heathrow Airport several times in the fog before giving up and diverting to Manchester. The bleak, grey weather was so very different to the dazzling desert conditions we had left behind. My father, sister and friends, who had driven down to London to meet us, now had to return to Wolverhampton while arranging for someone else to drive to Manchester to pick us up. Since this was long before mobile phones were invented, it was a complete logistical nightmare for everyone. The tarmac at Manchester Airport was packed full of diverted aircraft and there weren't enough passenger boarding stairs for all of us so we were left on the plane for what felt like hours, staring out of the windows at the rain. When we finally managed to disembark, the terminal was heaving with crowds of frustrated passengers and there were only two public telephones available for people to make whatever arrangements they needed to get home. It was a miserable homecoming in every possible way.

Then came three months of waiting for the baby to arrive while grieving for my lost husband and not knowing what I wanted to do with my life now that he was gone and I was going to be a mother. I was very grateful for my mother's practical support but it was still hard to be living in someone else's house, like a child, after having tasted the freedom of having my own home. It felt like I had been torn away from Jordan too quickly. Because of Muwaffaq, and because of the baby growing inside me, I still felt more rooted in Amman than I now did in Wolverhampton, but I couldn't see how I would be able to go back there once I was responsible for a child. Where would I live? How would I support myself and my child?

In the early hours of 1 March, my son was born at home with the doctor standing at the bottom of the bed happily puffing on cigarettes while the local midwife worked her magic. I didn't want to be in a hospital where all the other mothers would have the fathers of their babies gathering around their beds, while I would be all alone.

'When are you having him baptised?' the midwife asked.

'I'm not having him baptised,' I said.

'But he'll never go to Heaven,' she warned.

I called him Muwaffaq, because the name meant everything to me. In coming years this would prove to be a bit of a handicap for him, as it is not an easy name to pronounce. Ten days after the birth he was circumcised on the kitchen table. I don't know why I decided to say he was a Muslim, it just seemed the right thing to do, for his father and for his father's family. I wasn't religious, but they were. I knew it would mean a lot to them. I believed that all religions had caused a great deal of trouble in the world but for my mother-in-law, her religion was her only support, helping her to get through every day of her hard life. Believing that everything that happened to her was 'God's will', including the loss of her beloved eldest son, at least gave her something to cling on to.

King Hussein sent me a telegram of congratulations on the birth, adding that I had been provided with a house in Amman should I decide to return. This was the most wonderful news I could have hoped for, because at least that gave me something to build some plans around. It also confirmed in my mind that I didn't feel at home in England any longer, that I wanted to go back to the heat, the desert landscapes and the haunting sounds of the muezzins' calls to prayer. I immediately set about making plans but on 5 June 1967, the Six Day War broke out between Israel and a coalition of Arab states, including Jordan.

It was frustrating to be so far away from it all and to have to rely on the notoriously unreliable television and newspaper reports for my information, constantly trying to sort out fact from fiction, truth from propaganda. It soon became clear, however, that the Israelis had pulled off a stunning victory and that Jordan had lost the West Bank and Jerusalem, plus a huge amount of its armour and all its aircraft. By the end of the first day of the war, Jordan's air force had ceased to exist. Our pilots then went to Iraq and flew from there in Iraqi Air Force Hunters.

I heard that Firas Ajlouni, one of Muwaffaq's fellow pilots, had been killed when the Israelis attacked the air base at Mafraq while he was waiting to taxi for take-off. He was a lovely man who would occasionally give us a lift to Amman or back to Mafraq. He was a terrible driver and conditions on the road to Mafraq didn't help; it was only just wide enough for two cars to pass so meeting a lorry was always a problem, especially at night. The flashing of headlights would start from afar, becoming more urgent as we approached the oncoming vehicle and then becoming totally blinding as the full beams hit us, necessitating two wheels going into the ditch, two wheels remaining on the road and hoping for the best. Being a fearless and skilful fighter pilot, Firas was a great exponent of this art, at speeds which were nerve-racking in the extreme for his passengers. I knew the best solution was to close my eyes, but a perverse devil inside me always made them pop open at the last moment. Every time I thought this was the one we weren't going to survive but, in a swirl of dust, hooting and cursing, with half the car off the road, we always came through to live for the next encounter. It was hard to believe that such a powerful life force had been so easily snuffed out. Whenever I hear Procol Harum singing 'A Whiter Shade of Pale' I think of those rides with Firas.

His Majesty gave a speech to the United Nations on 26 June 1967, after the war. The following extracts demonstrate how wise and prescient he was.

> I will not speak to you only about peace, for the precondition of peace is justice. When we have achieved justice, we will have achieved peace in the Middle East. There has been much talk in these chambers about peace. There has been little talk about justice. Israel has stated that what its people want is peace and security. This has always been the cry of the successful aggressor – peace by submission of the victim and security for what he has. What Jordan and the Arabs want, on the other hand is peace with justice.
>
> Today's war is not a new war, but part of the old war, which will go on for scores of years if the moral and physical wrong done to the Arabs is not righted.
>
> Israel, I need not tell you, is a skilled adversary in the joint arts of concealed aggression and propaganda. Thus, it has lived in contempt for UN Resolutions and has lived in arrogant defiance of the UN for the past nineteen years. Each year, as the special committee meets to consider the extension of UNRWA's mission, the General Assembly reaffirms its moral positions, namely that the Palestinian Arabs should be permitted to return to their homes or else be compensated for their losses. And what has Israel done to honour this commitment? I need not answer the question.
>
> The Israelis are not a peaceful occupying force, but are engaged in destroying the homes and property of the

people. The Israelis' aim is clear – to make life so impossible for the Palestinians that they will never want to return. This is the policy she followed so successfully in 1948 and which she hopes to follow again.

What choice do the Palestinians have at the moment? Should they return to their homes and live under the military and political domination of people who are strangers to them, who speak a foreign language and who practice a new form of national and religious racism? Or, if they choose not to return, what choice is there but to become homeless exiles, doomed to spend a life without hope in the overcrowded Gaza Strip or on the Eastern Bank of the Jordan.

In October 1967, things calmed down and I returned, with my seven-month-old baby, to a Jordan that was in a state of shock from the aftermath of defeat and the loss of territory. Thousands of bewildered Palestinians were now living in tents. Only those who had lost their homes in 1948 were classified as refugees and came under the United Nations Relief and Works Agency (UNRWA). Those who lost everything in 1967, if they weren't already refugees, became 'displaced people'. This was because the West Bank in 1967 was part of the Kingdom of Jordan, so the rationale was that they had simply left one part of their country for another. Then there were those Palestinians who lived on the East Bank because of their work. They had also lost their homes and weren't able to go back to visit their families.

A few Jordanian pilots were training on the F104 in the USA when they were hastily recalled a few days before the war started. The family of one pilot I knew lived in a village on the West Bank, right on the border. His father said to him, 'if you are going to be shot, don't let it be in the back of your head, but in the front'. The Israelis kicked his family out of their home and blew it up in front of their eyes on the second day of the war. They were displaced and spent some time in a tent in a cemetery in Jordan before managing to find somewhere to live. Jordan slowly became overwhelmed with refugees and displaced Palestinians.

The house I had been given by the King was outside the main city of Amman, on a small estate that had been built for officers of the public security department. At that time, the estate consisted of two rows of one-storey limestone houses and all I could see on the surrounding hills was a mosque, a few other houses and the large army hospital. Everywhere else there were fields full of crops. Now, the city has spread over the whole area and you can hardly put a pin between the buildings.

Being back in Jordan was difficult for the first few months, having no car and trying to pick up all the threads of my life again, not just for me, but for my baby as well. Winter was approaching and the house had no central heating, so I bought a huge kerosene heater, which just warmed the main room. There were many low moments when I wondered if I had been crazy to come back, leaving my family support system behind in England.

On the first anniversary of Muwaffaq's death, I was feeling particularly depressed, when friends came over and brought me and the baby back to their house so I wouldn't feel lonely. Such little gestures meant the world. A few doors down the road, Glubb Pasha's son Faris lived with his wife Sharon and their son Mubarak. Sharon was a doctor and while she lived in Jordan she devoted herself to the medical care of refugees. We became good friends and life slowly settled into a pattern, but then another attack of hepatitis put me back in the hospital.

Once I was on my feet again, the King arranged for me to have a job in the air force, working in the commander's office, and gave me a car. One of my sisters-in-law found a young Palestinian girl from a refugee camp who came to live with me during the week and looked after

Muwaffaq while I was at work. Luckily, the hours weren't long and I could be home with him by 2.15 p.m. every day.

I was the only woman in the headquarters, which, of course, caused the usual problem – toilets! If I needed the facilities, I had to jump into my car and drive to my nearest friend, about five minutes away. The work was quite boring and was only enlivened when there would be arguments about what I thought should be written in English. I once refused to type an order which was addressed to 'Scotland, England'. It was difficult to explain that they are two separate countries, and it was a salutary reminder that the United Kingdom is not as much at the forefront of people's minds in other parts of the world as British people might like to think. Unless there is some direct connection, the rest of the world is as ignorant about us as we are about them. I had not known where Jordan was when first posted there, so why should I expect Jordanians to know anything about Britain?

During this time, I had my first trip in a helicopter. The air force flew the Alouette III, which was small but fun to fly in, especially if the pilot was someone you knew, and at moments like that, swooping over the desert hills, I felt I had made the right decision in returning.

The King would appear at my door quite often, just to see how I was doing or to chat about some project or other. He was easily bored and would just decide to go and visit someone without warning. On one of these visits, he turned up with a boot full of apples, bringing a crate into my kitchen.

'I've just come from the airport,' he told me. 'We gave some tanks to Lebanon and they've sent us apples in return.'

He always loved giving people gifts. One year he gave me a big Grundig radio, with an aerial, so I could get the BBC World Service, which he knew I loved listening to. He came around another day to find that Muwaffaq had ripped the aerial off.

'I'll get you another one,' he said, refusing to listen when I assured him it still worked just fine. I realised that it gave him pleasure to give me a new one, so I accepted graciously and, following his example, gifted the old one to a friend.

One day he came to see me and was looking for something to do, so I suggested that we go together to the room where all his gifts from visitors were stored, to sort it out a bit, which he thought was a good idea. As we looked around, I exclaimed at the beauty of two carved olive-wood figures and a silk cover from Damascus. Before the Syrian civil war started, Damascus was undergoing a lot of changes to help entice tourists. Wonderful boutique hotels were created in old buildings with courtyards and they cleared up the cables that festooned everything in the *souq*. One could wander for ages looking at all the fascinating things for sale, from rose petals and spices to carpets, glass works and clothing. The funniest shops were the ones selling female underwear, some of which sported feathers and flashing lights. They made wonderful joke birthday presents for female friends! It has been so sad to see this country being destroyed. Hopefully, now that the Assad regime has fallen, Syria will be able to rebuild.

'Take them,' the King said when he saw how much I liked the objects and I still have them today.

From time to time His Majesty, Princess Muna or one of the other royals would invite me to join them for a trip or an experience, particularly if they had other English visitors there, which meant that I got to meet some very interesting people. On one of these outings, I was sitting on the beach, talking to a dentist who had been flown out from London.

'I don't know who the dentist in England is for the Queen Mother,' I said, 'but her teeth are terrible, aren't they?'

'I am actually Her Majesty's dentist,' he replied.

'Oh,' I said, mortified at my faux pas.

'Too many gins and tonics and things like that,' he said, with a wry grin.

Sometimes Princess Muna's parents, Colonel and Mrs Gardiner, were also included in the royal party. The colonel was in the British army and had been working in Jordan on their water supplies when the King met his daughter on the set of the *Lawrence of Arabia* movie.

While I did a lot of socialising with the royal family, there were always history-changing events brewing in the background. On 21 March 1968, for instance, the Israelis pushed over the River Jordan and attacked a refugee camp near the village of Karameh. The Jordanian army and the Palestinians fought back and won a significant victory, but we were all deeply worried that the Israelis would push on up from the valley towards Amman. If that happened, could we defend ourselves? It was a nerve-racking day, with tanks rushing down to the valley, but then came the welcome news of the Israeli retreat and our lives could continue peacefully for a little longer.

9
Working for the King

WHEN THE KING'S SECRETARY left to go back to England, he generously offered me the job, which I was more than happy to accept. It was wonderful to work for His Majesty and much more interesting than working for the air force. Princess Muna had given him an amateur radio set for his birthday one year, so I became involved with sending cards to the many people he had spoken to over the airwaves. His was such an unusual call sign that when he went on the air there were always queues of people waiting to speak to him and to receive the coveted JY1 card with the crown on top.

Wayne, an American who His Majesty had made contact with, offered to come over to Jordan to clear as many calls as he could so that the King could have a more relaxing time speaking to other enthusiasts. He sat for hours at the radio and handled hundreds of calls. One day, His Majesty came into the room and Wayne didn't stand up, which I thought was surprisingly rude of him but once the King had left he confessed that he had split his trousers from the back to the front and couldn't get up without endangering his modesty.

I sometimes sat with the King while he was speaking on the radio and most of the time the people on the other end of the call had no idea who they were talking to and would ask for their best wishes to be passed on to the monarch. His Majesty wouldn't let on who was speaking and it was fun to imagine their shock when the JY1 card arrived through their door.

Whenever His Majesty had visitors, they were usually very nervous. If they were invited to his home, one of the Sudanese staff would come in with small glasses of tea, which had handles and saucers. Many times, I would hear the clatter of glasses against saucers as their hands shook with nerves.

One day, when Princess Muna was away in the Far East, His Majesty called me up to the house. When I got there, I found him with the prime minister, the chief of the royal court and some other important men. He was sitting at the end of the table, writing a speech and I joined them. We were all eating and talking when His Majesty suddenly dropped his pen and stood up.

'Come on, Trisha,' he said, 'let's go upstairs.'

I could feel myself turning as red as a beetroot, even though I knew perfectly well that, having finished the speech, he just wanted to get on his radio and talk to people around the world to take his mind off all the mayhem around him. I could quite imagine what it looked like to the other men around the table. Years later, I was chatting to the chap who was the chief of the royal court and he assured me that they didn't think anything of the incident but I'm sure he was just sparing my blushes.

On 1 August 1968, one of our fighter pilots got married. Hanna and his Armenian bride, Asdghig, had both been born in Jerusalem and were married in a Greek Catholic church in Amman. It wasn't like a church ceremony in the West, which is all very solemn. This was a festive and noisy affair. We all piled into our cars afterwards and drove around Amman, joyously hooting our horns before following the happy couple out to Mafraq for a party. This was another honeymoon that was going to be spent on the air base. Hanna had the dubious honour of being the first Jordanian Air Force pilot to bail out of an aircraft after only four hours of flying. He went on to fly Hunters and took part in the 1967 war when he was injured in an Israeli attack after landing in Amman. He finally retired as a brigadier in 1990 but sadly died of cancer. He and Asdghig were wonderful friends to me over the years.

•

The relationship between the Palestinian fedayeen and the ordinary citizens of Jordan began to deteriorate in 1968. The fedayeen became bolder and more intrusive and, in many ways, seemed to be taking control of the country. They set up checkpoints on the roads where you would be arbitrarily stopped and questioned. They roamed around the streets wearing masks, pointed guns out of car windows and would stride into hotels or restaurants, demanding money for their cause. I always refused to give in to such bullying tactics and if an argument ensued, I would tell them that my husband had died defending the West Bank which always put an end to the matter.

In later years, Muwaffaq's martyrdom was written about in all the history books and children learned about his death at school. Everyone in Jordan knew the story. There was even a graphic novel of the story produced, in which Muwaffaq is depicted looking like Dan Dare, the pilot from the old *Eagle* comics, and I look like a distressed Lois Lane. When I questioned the historical accuracy of these portrayals, the author merely shrugged and told me the book had been illustrated in Singapore as if that explained everything. Muwaffaq's legend has lived on to this day and a large air base, opened in 1981 in Azraq, is called the Muwaffaq Salti Air Base in his memory.

By the end of the 1960s, the atmosphere in the previously tranquil Amman had grown nasty and frightening. Jordan had done more for the Palestinians than any other Arab nation and it seemed like they were paying us back by trying to take over the country. From time to time the Israelis would fly over the city, dropping propaganda leaflets, just like they would over Gaza in 2023–24, increasing the feeling of impending doom for those of us trying to live normal, peaceful lives. As the levels of violence on the ground increased, many of the shops were fitted with metal shutters and at the first sound of gunfire, shop-keepers would rush outside to pull them down, the rattling sound reverberating around the rapidly emptying streets.

The Israelis then started launching air raids over Jordan, trying to hit fedayeen strongholds, dropping bombs and rockets all around us. The first warning we heard would be the mournful wail of sirens and, if in a car, we were then supposed to stop and jump into the nearest ditch, but I always preferred to drive straight home. The planes flew in so low that sometimes I could actually see the faces of the Israeli pilots as they swooped down over the roof of my house. Our anti-aircraft guns would then start firing and we would watch the skies, in a very matter-of-fact way, hoping to see an aircraft being hit as if we were watching a movie. It is frightening how differently one feels when the pilot is your enemy and not your husband. We believed they had no right to fly over our country, disrupting our lives with impunity and therefore deserved whatever fate befell them, whereas Muwaffaq had been defending Jordanian territory when he was shot down. To be honest, our feelings had nothing to do with politics or reason, it was purely an emotional response.

I was astonished at how aggressive my feelings had become as I had always been a very non-violent person. Was it revenge that I wanted? Did I hate the pilot who had shot my husband down? No, I didn't, but I did hate what the Israeli government was doing. I believe their policy of collective punishment has always been a hateful one, going against all human rights and conventions. It is a policy that they follow to this day and it is the reason I am still marching through the streets of London, more than fifty years later, demanding a ceasefire in Gaza and the creation of a Palestinian state.

I was staying in Aqaba in 1969 with His Majesty, family and friends, when reports came through of a fire at the twelfth-century Al-Aqsa Mosque in Jerusalem. The symbolism of the act looked for a while as if it could trigger a war, which could easily have spread until it engulfed the whole region. The incident led to riots and demonstrations all over the Muslim world before anyone knew the full story of what had happened. Luckily, it turned out that the fire had been started by an Australian Christian zealot who had set light to the pulpit and the news defused the situation before things got out of control. Al-Aqsa Mosque and the Dome of the Rock are situated on al-Haram al-Sharif and are the world's oldest surviving works of Islamic architecture, containing the earliest proclamations of Islam and the Prophet Muhammad. I still remember driving up the valley to Jerusalem in 1964 and seeing the Dome of the Rock for the first time. It personified Jerusalem and was the most amazing sight. I didn't realise at that time that I would only see it a few more times before the 1967 war. I was so privileged to see Jerusalem and all the holy sites.

Many years later, the golden dome was refurbished and His Majesty sold one of his houses in London to pay for the eighty kilos of gold required for the task.

By 1970, there seemed to be Iraqi troops, fedayeen and militiamen everywhere you looked around Amman. What were they all here for? As far as I could see, they were all aiming to destabilise Jordan for their own agendas, rather than pursuing their avowed desire of destroying Israel and it seemed that the fedayeen were gaining the upper hand in the chaos. The last thing the King wanted was a civil war and he went out of his way to accommodate all sides. It must have been very difficult for him to pacify the Jordanian army, who were outraged at what was happening. Some of them even had to travel to their units in civilian clothes and then change into their uniforms to avoid being attacked or shot, which they felt was humiliating in the extreme when they were in their own country.

At the beginning of June 1970, the fedayeen attacked the King while he was driving into Amman. He escaped, but the attempted assassination enraged the army.

I was stuck at the King's home when it happened. Princess Muna was in the Far East and only the four children were in the house (Princes Abdullah and Faisal and the twin princesses, Zein and Ayesha), along with their nannies. Although I was working right at the heart of the drama, the last thing we wanted to do was pester the King with questions, so it was often the wonderful BBC World Service that kept us informed about what was going on around us.

One night we were evacuated from the house, bundled into cars and taken on a hair-raising drive with no lights to an air raid shelter belonging to Prince Muhammad (the King's brother), where we all slept on mattresses, wondering what on earth the next day would bring. We eventually heard the news that the King had dismissed his uncle, Major General Sharif Nasser bin Jamil (Commander-in-Chief of the armed forces) and Brigadier Sharif Zeid Bin Shaker (another royal relative and the assistant chief of staff for operations) as the fedayeen felt that these two officers were out to destroy them. In fact, they were right to believe that. It was a blow that the King had to make concessions, but he didn't have the military strength to stand against the various factions at play. In time, when the moment came for him to let his army loose, they would be defeated. Uneasy lies the head that wears the crown, indeed. Most of the royal family were staying in London for their own safety, which must have been difficult for them when so much was happening in their home country. I eventually managed to get home from the shelter during a lull in the fighting without ever fully understanding what happened that night.

The families and wives of officers were having a particularly difficult time, especially the foreign wives. I was lucky enough to have a car, but most of the others didn't because their husbands had military transport and couldn't afford their own cars. This meant the women had to manage for themselves without transport, since the men were on duty most of the time.

Once the situation had calmed down, I went off to the United States to visit a wonderful couple called Charlie and Mary Ann Crider, who lived in Camp Hill, Pennsylvania. They had spoken to the King many times over the radio and he had invited them for a holiday to Jordan. They came over in the spring of 1970 and had a splendid time, hardly able to believe that they were in the company of a king and his family and they invited me back to stay with them in return. Their local paper even wrote an article about my visit, under the headline 'King's Gal Friday Visits in Camp Hill'.

> CAMP HILL – Mrs. Patricia Salti, quite blonde and still somewhat British, has one secretary's job that is decidedly embroidered with the stuff of adventure.
>
> She's personal secretary to King Hussein of Jordan.
>
> Visiting Mr. and Mrs. Charles G. Crider, of 105 June Dr., Mrs. Salti isn't a bit hesitant about conveying her enthusiasm for Hussein and Jordanians in general. She has good reason. In 1966, her husband, a young Jordanian fighter pilot was shot down by the Israelis.
>
> Mother of a small boy who lives with her parents in England, [he did not!] Mrs. Salti does not like to touch too firmly on the political meat and bones of Jordan's place in the Mid-east.

'King Hussein is a moderate,' she said, 'and I think his stand in the situation is right, and that's about all I can say.'

Mrs. Salti's correspondence deals principally with his contacts with ham radio operators throughout the world. And the radio is the reason Mrs. Salti is here. Crider happened to contact Hussein and Hussein invited the Criders to Jordan for a visit. The Criders made the trip last month, friendship developed with Mrs. Salti, thus Mrs. Salti is getting her first look at the United States.

The U.S.A. is a big hunk of country, she said. And she would not like to live here. 'There are these millions of people and there is this largeness that would be hard to cope with,' she said.

Mrs. Salti first went to Jordan as a staff member of the British Foreign Office, met her future husband and now, even as a widow, considers herself Jordanian-British.

She said Jordanians 'resent indeed' the pro-Israel stand of the United States. 'They judge all Americans by what they know of the American government,' said Mrs. Salti.

A woman of modesty, pleasant in manner and extremely intelligent, Mrs. Salti starts her return trip to Amman Monday.

As you can imagine, this flowery prose gave me, my family and pals a good laugh!

The journalist had obviously misunderstood about where Muwaffaq lived. My mother had been staying with me and she took Muwaffaq back to England with her so that I could make the trip to America. Mum and I had our ups and downs over the years, like most families, but she was always very supportive of me in my adventures and a dedicated grandmother to Muwaffaq. I picked him up on the way back to Amman. My son was becoming quite a handful as he grew up, but he loved spending time with his grandmother and the feeling was mutual. He was a handsome little fellow with a strong will of his own, which would grow a lot stronger over the years.

10

Refugee Wives

ON 1 SEPTEMBER 1970, the fedayeen again attempted to kill the King while he was on his way to the airport to meet Princess Alia, his daughter. His Majesty dove into a trench and a friend, who later became Prime Minister, jumped on top of him to protect him, which led to the King being more injured by his own ammunition belts than his would-be assassins. His Majesty then felt he had to retrieve his lost beret from the scene, which seemed an odd priority under the circumstances. Yet again, he survived the attack intact and returned to the palace amidst much cheering.

Then everything heated up with the hijacking by members of the Popular Front for the Liberation of Palestine of two airliners (one Swiss and one American) on 6 September and another (British) on 9 September. The planes were flown to Dawson's Field, an emergency airstrip in the desert, north-east of Zerqa.

Margaret Zahran (the wife of Michel, an air force engineer, but who would later marry my brother-in-law), Clare Shurdom (the wife of Ihsan at the time, a fellow fighter pilot of Muwaffaq's) and I decided things were becoming too dangerous and it was time to get our children out of the country. Margaret's boys were six-year-old Mazin and Nizar, who was eighteen months. Clare had three-year-old Tareq and Lisa, who was just eight months. Muwaffaq was three-and-a-half by then. We initially planned to drive the children up to Turkey, stay there until the situation had calmed down and then return. I had a Renault 16 and Clare had a large Volkswagen and we needed to get travel documents for the cars as well as for ourselves and the children. I don't know how we managed to do all the paperwork in time as we dodged around fedayeen check points, trying to keep away from the fighting, but we did. At that time smallpox certificates were also needed, but there we had to cheat and we paid for the certificates, without actually having the vaccinations.

We finally managed to get ourselves organised and with much trepidation we drove out of the city with nothing but an old atlas for a map, heading north just as a convoy carrying the hostages from the hijacked aircraft passed us on their way south into Amman. At that stage we didn't know that the Syrian army was massing on the Jordanian border, but we did know that the atmosphere in Syria wasn't very nice. I had my .38 Smith & Wesson revolver with me, though what I thought I was going to do with it I cannot imagine. The King had given it to me some time before and I had done a little target practice, even beating some of the men that I competed with, but I was definitely not comfortable with the idea of using it in a real-life situation.

Guns were very common in Jordan and often used at celebrations like weddings, as well as for fighting and killing. You would often hear volleys of shots going off into the sky as everyone cheered a bride and groom, a new graduate or a political speech. One Bosnian boy, who had come to Jordan in search of safety, was accidentally shot through the head when standing on a balcony above a wedding celebration. Some people's homes had guns casually lying about all over the place.

All through Syria we felt deeply uncomfortable and threatened, especially at a garage when we stopped for petrol. Maybe having so many small children with us protected us from getting into serious trouble.

We were painfully aware that if things became really nasty there was very little we could do to protect ourselves, even with the gun.

We spent one night in Damascus, then drove on up to the Turkish border. Once we got through, we stopped to sleep in İskenderun for a night. Small children, of course, don't care where they put their hands, so staying in places that didn't have any visible standards of cleanliness made us all completely paranoid. We took showers with our sandals on and hardly dared to even lie in some of the beds, imagining who had slept in them before us and what might be living in the filthy mattresses just waiting to emerge and bite in the night. We were exhausted, frightened and worried, with five little horrors who didn't understand what was going on around them or why their mothers were so tense. At least I didn't have a husband to worry about as well, like Clare and Margaret, and only one child.

I used to love going to Damascus as it was only a little over a four-hour drive from Amman. My mother-in-law was from Syria, so we had many relations there. It was a totally different country to Jordan. You never saw anything Western – no McDonald's, no Kentucky Fried Chicken. Totally poverty-stricken, it was under a totalitarian form of government but was always fascinating until it all turned to disaster. One of our Syrian cousins was in the Syrian Air Force. When he was visiting Amman in the 1960s, my husband and I were in the car with him when we stopped to buy some cigarettes (I never smoked, so not for me) and he pleaded with my husband not to leave him in the car with me as there were Syrian spies everywhere and to be seen with a foreigner was a complete no-no.

We arrived in Adana, in southern Turkey, the next day with no idea what to do next. Clare was beginning to think she might return to Amman but then the BBC announced that civil war had broken out in Jordan, so there was then no choice but to carry on. We drove through the beautiful Taurus mountains, across the long, dusty plain and into

Ankara, where we checked into the most expensive hotel we could find and just wallowed in hot baths and between clean sheets.

We thought the British embassy might be able to help us, but they were exceedingly uninterested. We heard that a boat was leaving Istanbul the next day and would be calling at Piraeus, Greece, en route to Genoa, the Italian port where I had first sailed away from Europe at the start of my grand adventure. We booked tickets and drove off towards Istanbul at top speed.

It was a race against time, taking much longer than we had been told, and we became increasingly convinced that we would miss the boat and be stranded in Istanbul. At last, with our nerves stretched to breaking point, we reached the Asian shore and looked across the fabled domes and minarets of Istanbul. We were standing on the very edge of Europe, but we had no time to appreciate any of the beauty or history as we frantically loaded the cars onto the ferry and crossed the Bosphorus, then disembarked and rushed to the docks to look for our ship. Every stage of the operation seemed to take forever, with everyone moving at snail-like speeds showing no sense of urgency. To our huge relief, the ship was still there as we dashed from one desk to another to get the paperwork done, trying to keep the children corralled as we went, wishing we had ropes to tie them to us as they wandered away in every direction. Finally, the cars were winched up and we staggered on board, all our energy drained and our nerves in shreds.

The ferry pulled away from the dock and only then did we have time to pause for breath and take in the conditions on the vessel that we were now trapped on. The hideous cabins were crawling with bed bugs, the communal toilets were overflowing with effluent and the food was beyond inedible. Above all else, there was the constant fear that one of the children would fall overboard. Even the best of friends would get tetchy in these circumstances, especially when the children started fighting with one another. So, we argued and felt annoyed with each other but somehow managed not to fall out completely.

We decided the boat was so awful we would get off at Piraeus, rather than continue on to Genoa, so I went up to my car on the deck just before docking to get prepared. A nice elderly man strolled over to chat.

'Are you getting off here?' he asked.

'Yes.'

'Would you be kind enough to take this tin in your car, as it is so heavy? I will come and collect it after we have landed.'

'Of course,' I said, feeling sorry for the poor old guy and too distracted to think straight. 'That's fine.'

We landed and the cars were craned down. The customs officers came over and ordered us to empty them so that they could inspect everything for contraband. They then realised, as they saw the children milling around our legs, that the piles of nappies, toys and rubbish would take hours to lift in and out, so they decided just to glance through the windows instead.

Unfortunately, their eyes immediately alighted on the tin, which was sitting in clear view, waiting for its owner to claim it and I could feel myself flushing alternately hot and cold as I saw the whole scenario through their eyes and realised the enormity of my mistake. How could I have been so stupid? Obviously, the old guy was not as innocent as he had seemed and I had allowed myself to fall for one of the oldest tricks in the smuggler's handbook. Was I now going to end up in a Greek prison? Taking a deep breath, I explained what had happened and pointed out the man who had asked me to take the tin who was skulking near the gate, watching the proceedings and feigning casual innocence.

Thankfully, the customs officials took pity on us and were very understanding. They could obviously see that three harassed young mothers didn't have the capacity to be into any sort of smuggling, so they simply took the tin away and waved us through. It was a mistake

I would never make again and I have often wondered what was in that tin – drugs? Olive oil?

Safely into Greece, we now needed to ponder our next move but first we had to find somewhere for the children to sleep that night. We headed to Glyfada Beach, about half an hour's drive away and checked into some chalets on the beach – such luxury after what we had endured on the ship. The only money we had was four hundred Jordanian dinars in cash (about £800), which the King had given to me to buy something or other for him, so we needed to change them into Greek currency. That very day, however, the banks stopped dealing in the Jordanian dinar because of the outbreak of civil war. Our cash had suddenly become worthless. Now, we didn't have any money to pay the hotel bill for the previous night, let alone to continue our travels. The prospect of being thrown into a Greek prison loomed into my mind once more.

I called my parents in England to explain our plight and my father gave me the name and address of his company's representative in Athens. I asked them to transfer some money out to us, which they were more than happy to do but at that time there were restrictions on the amount of money that could be taken out of the UK without the express permission of the Bank of England. My mother and sister went up to the Ottoman Bank in London to try and arrange for a transfer and, as luck would have it, they found a member of staff reading a copy of the *Daily Express*, dated 21 September, and there we were on the front page, our story having been given to them, probably by Clare's mother.

Under the headline 'REFUGEE WIVES AND THE TINY TOTS TAKE THE LONG ROAD HOME' was a large picture of Clare and Tareq. This little bit of media fame was enough to persuade the bank that our need was genuine and urgent and they agreed to transfer some money out to us.

Now that we could resume our journey, we decided to drive to Patras and catch a boat from there to Brindisi, in Italy, stopping off at Corfu on the way. To our relief, this boat proved to be quite civilised and we were beginning to feel more comfortable as we sat on deck and breathed in the warm sea air. Once we were back on dry land, we then drove up through Italy, breaking our journey by staying with a friend of Clare's in Milan. The drive was exhausting, especially as baby Lisa had now fallen ill. Poor Clare was having to deal with a sick baby in a foreign country while driving and coping with fractious children and cranky fellow travellers. Her friend in Milan, however, looked after us well until we were able to put our cars onto a train to Ostend in Belgium. As we boarded the train, we thought that we had a whole compartment to ourselves, but to our horror another couple joined us. They only spent a few minutes with us, however, before they realised that three harassed mothers and five ghastly children were not going to be the best of travelling companions and beat a hasty retreat.

At Ostend we boarded yet another ferry and a few hours later we saw the white cliffs of Dover on the horizon. I think, at that moment, we all cried.

11

Life in England

My parents had just moved south from the Midlands and were living in a rented flat in Maidenhead, Berkshire, before moving into their new house. Margaret's parents lived in South London, so she called her brother and we arranged to drop her off on the way. After driving all the way from Jordan without any navigational problems, I found the English road system very confusing and the signs didn't help. Even after being given detailed instructions, we kept getting lost. Maybe exhaustion was playing a part in our confusion.

Eventually, however, we made it and, having said goodbye to Margaret, Mazin and Nizar, and their two huge suitcases, which had driven us mad throughout the journey, Clare and I set off again towards my parents. They didn't have room for all of us in the flat, so Clare stayed the night in a hotel and the next day headed for Lincolnshire, where her mother lived.

After a couple of days, I took my gun to the nearest police station, where they nearly had a fit, telling me I could be sent to prison for ten years for smuggling it into the UK. I even received a letter from the chief constable, rebuking me for my carelessness. In fact, I had completely forgotten I had the gun and only remembered it when I was cleaning out the car and found it in the glove compartment.

So began another new phase of my life. My parents and two sisters, myself and Muwaffaq, moved into the new house in Holyport in Berkshire. I had no idea what I was going to do with the rest of my life, but for now I wanted to concentrate on being a good mother to Muwaffaq.

I still couldn't decide if I should bring my son up in England or Jordan, so in March 1971, I went back to Amman on my own to see if I could work out the best place for us to be. By that time Margaret had also returned, so I was able to stay with her. Although the major conflict was over by then, there was still sporadic fighting and shooting and the whole city felt uncomfortable and unstable. That made my mind up. It was not going to be a good place to bring up a small boy for the next few years, so I returned to live for the foreseeable future in England. Having made the final decision, my house in Amman was bought off me by the Palace for 7,000 dinars (equal to about double that in pounds), although I only received £7,000. It was another kind gesture by the King and the house was given to Ihsan and Clare. With that money I was able to buy a flat in Windsor, just down the road from my parents, where Muwaffaq and I then lived for the next eleven years. I was supposed to get more money than actually arrived, but somehow a portion of it disappeared into someone else's pocket along the way. I later discovered that everyone in Jordan had heard on the grapevine that His Majesty had bought me a house for 35,000 dinars, which was a complete fabrication as my flat cost £7,450! There was always so much gossip around the King and his family, it was hard to separate fact from fiction.

I didn't have to get a job in England as I found I could just about manage on the monthly allowance that His Majesty awarded me as the widow of a martyr and I was more than happy with that, as I wanted to be around for Muwaffaq's early years. His Majesty also agreed to pay for Muwaffaq to attend private school, firstly at Papplewick Prep

School in Ascot and then at Harrow, one of the most famous public schools in the country, where the King and a number of other wealthy Jordanians had been educated. It was an enormously generous offer, which I didn't hesitate to accept, although I did find it embarrassing to have to ask His Majesty and I confessed my embarrassment to his personal assistant in the UK, who very kindly put it all into perspective for me.

'Don't worry, Trisha,' she assured me, 'one term's fees at Harrow are no more than two weeks' food from Harrods.'

In 1975, some good friends in Amman, Hilmi (an army anaesthetist) and his wife Betty, borrowed a large Winnebago camper from the King's garage. They asked if Muwaffaq, who was eight years old at the time, and I would like to join them and their three children (Yasmin, David and Janine), driving from Jordan to England. I guess by then the uncomfortable memories of my last trip along that route were fading and nostalgia was making me hanker for another adventure on the open road. So, I accepted the offer and Muwaffaq and I flew out to Amman to join them.

We packed the camper and set off in high spirits. About twenty kilometres down the road, we had our first breakdown, when the fan belt went. Hilmi might have been the most brilliant anaesthetist around, but he certainly was not a great car mechanic and we continued to break down with regular monotony throughout the journey.

Damascus was painfully hot when we arrived and we parked at the Syrian army's officers' mess. The next day the camper refused to start once again and United Nations personnel had to come to our rescue. At the same time, Betty and I were both beginning to feel unwell. Once we were back on the road, we took the route that I had driven in 1970. This time, at least, someone else was concentrating on the driving and I was able to take in the full beauty of the countryside we were travelling through. The children, on the other hand, didn't seem to take much notice of anything going on outside the camper's windows, spending all their time giggling and playing, so I was quite surprised when they talked about the trip later and had many more memories than we imagined they would. For me it was a fascinating journey, despite the fact that I felt terribly ill on and off throughout the whole trip. When I was still feeling ill, weeks later, I went to see a variety of doctors, none of whom could find anything wrong with me until one day, once we were back in Windsor, I decided I couldn't go on any longer and took myself back to the doctor and was then sent to hospital. After various tests it was found I had giardia, which is a tiny parasite usually carried in dirty water. Once identified, it was quickly cured with antibiotics. I just wished it could have been diagnosed sooner.

The urge to keep going back to Jordan didn't fade, however long I was away. A couple of years later, my brother-in-law, Muhammad, decided he wanted to buy a car in Germany and drive it to Jordan. He asked if I would like to go with him for the ride. Ignoring all my reservations and all the warning voices in the back of my head, I couldn't resist the offer. It was like some invisible force kept on drawing me back to Amman, the city where I had enjoyed my greatest adventures as well as my greatest tragedy.

We flew to Frankfurt and Muhammad bought himself a Volkswagen. The trip was to be a fast one and we shared the driving as we travelled through Austria, Yugoslavia, Bulgaria, Turkey and Syria, following a different route to my previous trips. Bulgaria was horrid and I decided that if I ever found myself in conversation with someone who thought communism was a good idea, I would advise them to go there and see just how grim the reality could be.

We were stopped by the police in Turkey who looked at our passports and asked, 'How many children do you have?'

'One,' I said.

'Two,' Muhammad said at the same time.

After a lot of confused mumbling between us, we decided the easiest thing was to settle on two. For the purposes of border control it was easier for us to pass as a married couple. Hotel accommodation also proved to be quite funny. Double rooms were so much cheaper than singles so we would ask for a room with single beds and then move them as far apart as possible. Luckily it was only for a few nights.

Muhammad wanted to stay in Damascus, so when we got there, at about four o'clock in the afternoon, I found a taxi that was heading for Amman. There were five other passengers in the car and after a while, the driver decided that he would put the fare up. Unsurprisingly, not everyone agreed with this blatant bit of extortion, so he pulled over to the side of the road and refused to move until everyone had given in and paid up. We were in a no-win situation, which he knew only too well. Things remained tense as we drove on through the evening.

There were no problems at Dera'a, on the Syrian border, but we had dropped off one of the male passengers before we got to the border post. By the time we were driving through no man's land on the other side, it was dark and the same man appeared in our headlights at the side of the road. The driver pulled over and the man jumped back into his seat, obviously by prior agreement. I had the same sinking feeling as when I realised I had accidentally become a smuggler on the dockside in Piraeus, all those years before. If he had to avoid the Syrian border post, I wondered, who was he and what had he done? Who was going to be after him? Were we about to become a target? Would whoever was after him think that the rest of us were involved in whatever he was up to? My head was buzzing with potentially catastrophic scenarios. We drew up at the first Jordanian checkpoint and my heart was thumping in my ears. I could hardly breathe. The guards examined our passports and then pounced on our suspicious fellow traveller, dragging him off to an unknown fate. Our driver put his foot down and we sped away, never to find out who he was or what he had been up to, just glad that we were not in trouble by association.

There was then a long delay at Ramtha and I was feeling totally exhausted, having left Ankara with Muhammad at dawn that day. It was now past midnight. I tried to persuade the driver to drop me off first, when we got to Amman, but he insisted on leaving me until last. That meant I would be alone in the car with him in the middle of the night. I thought my last moments were approaching and couldn't get myself together to make a rational decision. Nobody in Jordan knew I was coming that day, so nobody would notice if I never arrived. In my exhausted state, I was once again envisaging the darkest and most catastrophic outcomes possible.

But then I was dropped off, all in one piece, at the entrance to the King Hussein Medical Center (the large army hospital complex) and the driver accelerated away into the night. The soldier on duty was obviously surprised to have a foreign woman dumped on his doorstep in the middle of the night on her own, but he showed me to a telephone and I was able to call Hilmi, who came down to collect me. I was so relieved to be there safely, and I have never been tempted to do another solo trip in a car full of strangers.

•

I wanted Muwaffaq to get a good education and to learn to be independent, which was why I asked for His Majesty's help with the school fees, but I am not sure how happy he was during those school years or whether I made the right decision by sending him to board. Does any parent ever know if they have done the right thing by their children? I hope my son will forgive me if he thinks I made any wrong decisions.

I had never believed in boarding schools, and thought children were always better off living at home with their families, but as the only child of a single parent, I wanted Muwaffaq to be able to stand on his own two feet without being reliant on a clingy mother. Papplewick was a lovely school and he was a day boy there until the age of eleven, when they insisted that all the boys board until they went on to their big schools at the age of thirteen so that boarding would not be too big a shock to their system. On the one hand, I was loath to be parted from Muwaffaq when he was still so young, but on the other I had been warned by other single mothers that it was all too easy to become so embroiled in your child's life that when they grow up and leave home you are left with no life of your own. The first time I dropped him off to board I cried my eyes out once I got home, even though the school was only a couple of miles down the road and I was able to go and watch him in rugby and cricket matches, and any other activity that parents could be part of. Perhaps it was a good way of preparing me for the transition to Harrow, as well as him.

As he grew older, Muwaffaq and I started to clash more often. One day, when he was about twelve, I had my hair permed and it was all very curly, instead of my usual straight style. Arriving at Papplewick to pick him up, I dashed upstairs where I was told he was playing table tennis. I put my head through the door.

'Come on,' I said, 'it's time to go.'

He came downstairs without a word and with a face like thunder. He got into the car and slammed the door angrily,

'Mum,' he said, 'don't ever do that to me again. You look like something from outer space!'

I guess children don't like their parents to change.

When Muwaffaq was eleven or twelve, a pal and I thought we would take our children to the theatre for a bit of culture. The Oxford Playhouse was showing *The Return of A.J. Raffles* by Graham Greene, about the famous gentleman thief. Within minutes of the curtain going up, a naked lady appeared on the stage. Lyn and I looked at each other, then at the boys, whose eyes were out on stalks. It was not what we had expected.

'That was very rude, Mummy,' Lyn's daughter piped up at the interval.

I also took Muwaffaq to see *Waiting for Godot* by Samuel Beckett in which, infamously, absolutely nothing happens. Muwaffaq still talks about it as the most boring theatrical experience he has ever had.

Harrow was a different kettle of fish to Papplewick. Steeped in history, the school had a wonderfully quaint aura. The boys lived in various houses dotted around Harrow Hill and wandered about in straw boaters and black suits. When I took my brother-in-law to visit one day, he was visibly shaken. Knowing that His Majesty and other members of the Jordanian royal family had attended the school, he had expected to see something resembling a five-star hotel rather than the very spartan living conditions I showed him. The Park, where Muwaffaq lived, has since been renovated, so I trust the boys have better facilities now.

At his first Harrow Speech Day, Muwaffaq sang a solo in front of about six hundred parents. My father, mother and I were overcome with pride and emotion, sitting in the audience. He had a lovely voice and got to sing in both Salisbury and Winchester cathedrals. Once his voice broke, however, it was never the same again.

By chance I met up with an old friend, Sharon Glubb, (her husband, Faris, was Glubb Pasha's son). Their son Mark (Mubarak) was also at the school so Sharon and I were able to renew our friendship, which was a nice connection with the past and a time in my life that I looked back on with great affection.

The years I spent in England were not unhappy, but they were not fantastic either and I just couldn't see a long-term future for myself there, whereas in Jordan I had a lot of good friends and a lot of connections that could lead to much more interesting jobs than anything I was likely to be offered in the UK now that I was thinking of going back to work. I just felt that there were more things I could do with my life there.

I had a few romantic affairs after being widowed at twenty-four, but none of them turned into long-term relationships, which I am quite relieved about now, looking at some of my friends' relationships and partners. One of my affairs left me with a sore heart when it ended, but everything passes and I never met anyone who had as powerful an effect on me as my husband did. The only thing I miss about not having a partner is having someone to come home with after being in company and being able to have a good gossip about everyone else.

When we were on another holiday in Jordan in 1982, I finally decided that I wanted to come back to live in Amman. The country had always drawn me and I never really stopped thinking about my earlier times there. Muwaffaq was fifteen by then and becoming increasingly independent. Our relationship was very up and down, but he was doing well at school, having achieved ten O levels. He was now working for his A levels and would soon be an adult with no need for his mother, especially as he would have my mother there in England for support if needed.

The move was made and Muwaffaq would come to Amman in the school holidays. He seemed to have plenty of friends in the city. In fact, I hardly saw him when he was there because he was always out partying. When he was in England, he would often see my parents, although my father died in 1982 at the age of sixty-two and my mother then moved down to Poole to be nearer to my youngest sister Ann. She would still go to all his school events whenever I was not in England. They were very close and she was always there to cheer him on.

Having decided that Amman would be my home again. I just needed to work out how to support myself financially.

12

Help from the King

A LOT HAD CHANGED in Jordan in the eleven years I had been away. King Hussein had divorced Princess Muna and married Queen Alia, who died in an helicopter crash in 1977. A year later, he married Queen Noor. The King's generosity hadn't changed, however, and on my return His Majesty helped me to find a house and gave me a new Mercedes so that I could get around. Meanwhile, other people I knew started to give me small jobs to do. I bought a couple of typewriters and a friend and I typed out telephone directories to get a bit of cash coming in. I had managed to find a tenant to rent my flat in Windsor before leaving England, so that also provided me with a small, but regular, income.

I was confident that His Majesty would find something more permanent for me to do, but he had a great many more important matters on his plate, so I knew I had to wait patiently for him to contact me. In the days before mobile phones, waiting for a call from someone as busy as the King meant that you basically had to stay home in order not to miss it when it came. There was one suggestion that I should work in the queen's office. That didn't happen, but other opportunities came along and in 1984 I was working a few hours a week in the General Headquarters. I also helped organise several of the royal family's weddings, including that of the daughter of Sharif Zeid, who was commander of the armed forces. For the first wedding I was working with the English society hostess, Lady Elizabeth Anson, who I didn't get on with at all well and after that with Sir Michael Parker, who was the organiser of the Royal Tournament in England, as well as innumerable royal events and celebrations for Queen Elizabeth, Prince Philip, Prince Charles and Princess Diana. Michael and I got on very well indeed. His ideas were always incredibly imaginative, although often quite hard to execute, and he taught me a great deal. I remember at one wedding we filled a swimming pool with rocks and plants to make it look like a beautiful, natural lake. Getting the rocks out again, once the festivities were over, however, was quite a challenge.

I first met Michael when he came to Jordan to see how the Jordanian Armed Forces Band would work in the Royal Tournament in London. I then travelled to London with the band, to help them with their PR and any problems and to liaise with Michael and the production team. It was an amazing experience and I learned so much. We chartered a plane to take the band and also 'Glubb's Girls' (the Bedouin Camel Corps) in all their finery. When we landed at RAF Lyneham in England, we realised that the bullets the soldiers had in their belts were all live and would have to be confiscated. For three weeks, I attended every performance of the Tournament and got to sample just how well the British army feeds and looks after its people. Michael then came back out to Jordan to organise a military show for His Majesty's birthday, complete with daylight fireworks. A special area had to be found with spectator stands built. It was all such fun, but very stressful at the same time. We went around all the various arms of the armed forces looking for those who could contribute – including the army, the air force, the police, the horses, the camels and the motorbikes. Michael then put a programme together and began rehearsing. I stood next to Michael doing the timekeeping for each act. 'Don't forget,' he always said, 'on the day, the adrenaline will be pumping and the acts will happen more quickly, so factor that into all your calculations.'

Even though everything was organised to the split-second, just like a real military operation, things still went wrong. During the rehearsals, a man fell out of a helicopter and was killed instantly. Michael was brilliant at staying totally calm under pressure. For the first show there were huge nets behind each side of the main entrance gate for hundreds of balloons to be released at the end of the show. I had arranged for helium pipes to be set up with masses of nozzles for the soldiers to be able to blow up the balloons. We went off for lunch and when we came back found the majority of the balloons lying on the ground instead of floating at the top of the nets. The soldiers said that it was much quicker to blow them up themselves instead of using helium! Another time, Michael ordered a flag with the measurements of twenty metres by ten metres, to be hoisted by two fire engines with telescopic ladders. We were waiting at the Civil Defence HQ for the flag to arrive so that it all could be rehearsed when an army motorbike arrived and handed over a smallish envelope – they thought a mistake had been made and it should be two metres by one metre. There were so many funny stories. I had so much fun, as well as stress, and learned such a lot about how to run these amazing military shows.

At one show the brigadier in charge of everything made a speech when His Majesty arrived with the president of Egypt. It was all timed down to the second as there was going to be a fly-past when the speech ended. The brigadier, however, decided to lengthen his speech without telling anyone, so the fighter planes flew over exactly on time but drowned out the end of the speech. Serve him right for deciding unilaterally to lengthen his speech with no reference to the producer.

Many years later, when the military show was being staged without Michael and his team, I was asked to help with the timings. The job is relatively easy if the performances are all being staged on the ground, but if you have an air force and helicopters to synchronise, things become more complicated. Having sat next to the master (Michael) so many times, however, I was becoming quite the expert. It was still completely nerve-racking, especially when things went wrong, although in most cases the audiences never noticed that anything was amiss. One of the royal guards, who should have cued us on the arrival of His Majesty at the rear entrance of the arena, didn't. His Majesty arrived three minutes early and the first we knew was when we saw him appear in the royal box – so there was no twenty-one-gun salute or trumpet fanfare and I was frantically recalculating all the timings.

I never really had a full-time job title at this stage, I was more of a 'Jill of all trades', seeking out interesting things to do and then finding ways to get paid for doing them. I am a very organised person, although I'm sure there were plenty of people who thought I just liked interfering in everything interesting that was going on. I happened, for instance, to be passing through the airport when I saw Annette Yarrow, a visiting sculptress, and her photographer husband, looking a little lost. When I enquired if she was okay, she admitted that she had arrived to organise the siting of a life-sized bronze statue of a Bedouin on a horse from the time of the Arab Revolt in 1917, which was a present for His Majesty from the armed forces and she wasn't quite sure how to proceed. This was exactly the sort of problem I enjoyed sorting out and the statue now stands proudly in Parliament. Annette also gave me a miniature reproduction in bronze as a thank you for my assistance.

I also worked with the Jordanian Armed Forces Band, which plays at special occasions and includes the bagpipes. In the 1990s, the Austrian government offered to form an orchestra from the Armed Forces Band, with training in classical music in Vienna. It wasn't easy for a trumpet player or a bagpiper to suddenly train in classical music with their only language being Arabic, let alone to spend three years in Vienna. Yushka Birkus-Kigo had been a conductor in Vienna and he came to Jordan with his wife Hannelore to help set up the orchestra after the training had finished. We became friends and I became a confidante and learned about all their problems, which could be hilarious or depressing. Once, when giving a concert in front of His Majesty and the royal family, Yushka went out for a quick cigarette and the royal guards wouldn't allow him back in. He nearly missed the concert.

David Attenborough came out to Jordan to film for a series called *The First Eden*, investigating the history of mankind's relationship with the natural world in the lands around the Mediterranean. He was using police horses for filming out in the desert, so I helped organise that and got a chance to spend time with this fascinating man. I also spent time with a British general who came out to make training videos for the armed forces.

On another occasion I got to look after some very wealthy Jewish visitors from the USA, including the famous television journalist, Barbara Walters, who went on to interview His Majesty. Somehow, she engineered that she and I would be walking alone along the *Siq*, a narrow passage leading to the famous Treasury in Petra.

'If you give me the low-down on His Majesty,' she said, 'I'll tell you some things about Hillary Clinton.'

I declined the offer and later I overheard her talking about me, saying, 'that woman's not interested in anything!' That made me even happier that I had not agreed to barter gossip with her. His Majesty and the rest of the royal family had been so open and kind to me through the years, I would never have dreamed of betraying their confidences to anyone, least of all a journalist.

I helped to organise a conference on education for someone else I met and I worked in the army headquarters two or three times a week. I became involved with the Martyrs' Memorial museum, a huge, beautiful square building, with a black strip all around it framing quotations in gold from the Koran, and a courtyard at the top, bearing the names of all the martyrs, including, of course, my husband. A wonderful, huge painting by Terence Cuneo hangs there, depicting the defence of Jerusalem in 1948.

I was delighted when the commander of the air force told me he wanted to publish a book of the history of the Royal Jordanian Air Force for public relations purposes and asked if I would be willing to help. I have always been fascinated by air forces and aeroplanes, which was perhaps one of the reasons I was first attracted to Muwaffaq. During our marriage I would sometimes help him with his maps because I was so interested. In the late 1980s, I had started researching the history of the RJAF by talking to all the pilots I knew. Gradually, my interest spread to cover all military aviation in the area and I began visiting the Public Record Office at Kew whenever I was in London. I found I really enjoyed the process of researching.

'What do you want for doing this work?' the commander asked.

'Nothing,' I replied, 'except that my name is in the book.'

He agreed and we set to work, with the help of a pal who was a brigadier. It soon became obvious, however, that the air force didn't hold many historical documents and it was also clear that a committee was not able to contribute much to the process. So, the brigadier and I did all the interviewing and researching, reading masses of books on Middle Eastern wars, and I then wrote the text. Many of the pictures we managed to borrow from private collections. No one wanted to lend them to the air force as so many had been lost in the past, but we managed to persuade them.

Many of the pilots I interviewed were personal friends, so it was enormous fun, but I was learning that you can never rely too much on people's memories and I always double-checked with flying logbooks whenever it was possible. I flew in a Casa C-212 (a twin-engine small aircraft) to an air base to photograph pilots with their Mirage aircraft and then two days later, in a C-130 around Amman. When we landed, one of the mechanics showed us a long kite string wrapped around one of the propellers – which shows how low we were flying. There were, in fact, some complaints because C-130s are not usually allowed to fly low over the city. I have to admit I felt a bit queasy on some of the tighter turns. Then, we got this beautiful Falcon named Selman from the desert police and I asked a dear friend, Jane Taylor, to photograph it at the RJAF base in Amman. We then went out to Muwaffaq Salti Air Base to photograph some Hawk missiles, with fighter aircraft flying over, which was harder than it sounds because those aircraft whip by in split-seconds. Andrea Atallah did a wonderful job of designing the book and I was sorry that she had to be embroiled in all the nonsense that followed.

In the early stages of the project, I was told that I could not include some material about the defection of Jordanian pilots and aircraft to Egypt during the Yemen crisis in 1962. I argued fiercely that the story should be there because it was part of the history, but the air force weren't to be persuaded and in the end I had to concede.

Then the commander was replaced and the project fell to pieces. I was very shaken and upset at all that transpired. The new commander wanted to take the whole project out of my hands and I felt that I had been treated with a total lack of respect and put in an invidious position. The book was ready for printing and in all my years in Jordan I had never been treated in such a manner. I asked for assurances that my name and the names of those who had also worked on the book would appear and that I would be totally involved in all the decisions around any changes to it. I said that until those conditions were met, I would hold on to all the materials, which I then stored in a safe place in one of the offices in the palace. There was a huge amount of pressure put on me to give them the material. The new commander tried to get the materials back by complaining about me to everyone he could think of (one of whom being the head of military intelligence, who was a pal of mine) but he didn't succeed. He also said I was trying to control everything, and the air force! He then created and printed an alternative book himself, which turned out to be rubbish.

After another change of commander, and with one last tussle, my version of the book was finally printed locally and I spent a lot of time at the printers making sure that everything was done properly. The printing went ahead and when they called to tell me it was finished, I collected ten hardbacks and ten paperbacks. I then received a call from the printers, asking me to return them as the air force was refusing to receive their order if it was twenty books short. By that stage I had run out of patience and I ignored them. The whole process had been a saga of disappointment, but the final book looked great and my research has since been used in other books on Middle Eastern air forces, which makes me very proud.

I also helped Princess Alia, His Majesty's eldest daughter, with organising her horse show. I had always loved horses and riding, right from when my parents bought me a horse as a girl, living in Wolverhampton. When I first arrived in Jordan I would ride out into the desert in the cool of the mornings with another girl on horses from the polo stables. There was one horse in the polo stables that I particularly liked, called 'Magic Carpet', which seemed a very apt name for the romantic setting in which we were riding. Later, I would ride horses from the royal stables.

Not all the sights I saw, of course, were so romantic. This was back in 1964 and once when driving home through the centre of town, I saw three bodies hanging from gibbets in front of the mosque. It was a huge shock and I tried not to look and to put it out of my mind. Jordan still has the death penalty, although it is not used very much, but I never saw a sight like that again.

Many of the jobs that I was assigned started out as my own ideas, so many of them were really interesting projects to work on. Sometimes, of course, I still had to take on tedious administrative work just to get some money in. I was always apprehensive about the state of my finances, worrying how I was going to manage as I grew older and less able to find work. From the moment I left the British embassy, I was living on the edge all the time, never having any long-term security. But then, none of the career paths which would have offered security ever seemed remotely interesting to me.

Muwaffaq got a student pilot's licence and flew solo for the first time, which was thrilling, reminding me of my time with his father. He thought he might like to join the British army and I arranged for him to go to Cyprus in order to get some practical experience.

One day, Prince Hassan asked me what my son was studying at university. When I told him 'a master's in Economics', he said, 'oh good, he can come and work for me.'

'No, he can't Sidi,' I said, a little too quickly, 'he needs to earn enough to look after his mother in her old age, not to mention supporting a wife and family. He could never afford all that on the sort of salaries you pay.'

He laughed, as if I were joking but it was undoubtedly true.

One of the advantages of working for royalty was getting to meet interesting people, including members of the Hashemite family, most notably King Hussein himself.

Brought up in a dysfunctional family, he came to the throne at the age of seventeen and survived numerous plots against him, becoming a great statesman and advocate for peace and justice in the Middle East. A British ambassador described him perfectly in this despatch:

> In the midst of all this excitement, the two young kings sat side by side, evidently great friends, though in complete contrast to each other. King Feisal, red-cheeked, easy of manner, with a Savile Row suit and a Curzon Street type of haircut, made King Hussein, dressed by a tailor in the

Salt Road, (the main street), and barbered by someone from the Suq, appear by comparison the country cousin, which he literally is. Yet there could be no doubt which was the stronger personality. King Feisal looked like an agreeable young English cavalry officer sitting beside a haggard, dynamic Bedouin prophet.

He was an amazing man, who crossed so many bridges and faced so many obstacles. I met royalty from many other countries, which was always fascinating. Some were nice, like the lovely Duchess of Edinburgh, who insisted I call her Sophie, and some were not so nice!

When Muhammad Daoud, a goat herder near Jerusalem, saw the biplanes of the RAF flying overhead he vowed to join up himself. He enlisted in 1944 as an aircraft mechanic at RAF Lydda Air Force Base in Palestine and when the RAF withdrew, he went to Jordan to enlist in the new Arab Legion Air Force, working on the plane (a Dove) that was designated to be King Abdullah I's private aircraft. When the king was assassinated on 20 July 1951, in Jerusalem, the aircraft had been positioned at Kolundia Airfield for the flight back. Sadly, they brought back his body instead. Muhammad was a delight to sit and chat to. He told me what happened that day and I have his written memories.

I met the pilots of the RAF Red Arrows aerobatic teams who came to Jordan annually to display, and the pilots of the Frecce Tricolori of the Italian Air Force. Sitting next to one of the Italian pilots after their display at the RJAF Mafraq base, he asked me who I thought was the better team – luckily, I had a good answer ready: since the Italians give a crazy display and the Arrows are so precise, they aren't really comparable.

My father supplied Chubb fire equipment for the international air shows at RAF Greenham Common and he told us they were always on red alert when the Italians were flying.

The Red Berets of the British army tried to persuade me to do a tandem parachute drop, but I was too much of a coward to accept the challenge.

In 1997 I met Professor David Kennedy and later Dr Bob Bewley, both aerial archaeologists. I was able to introduce them to people who could help them and to find out about a branch of archaeology I had never heard of before. It was fascinating to see how taking pictures from the air, and using Google Earth, unveiled so much information. Luckily, Jordan has been very open to aerial archaeology, which has provided an amazing insight into the past.

Over the years I have met many wonderful people from different UN agencies and various charities and I always admire their dedication and hard work.

I have been able to enjoy so many wonderful experiences, like taking the lovely Patti Boulaye to the Roman Theatre downtown and hearing her sing to an empty auditorium, appreciating how clever the Romans were with their acoustics as her voice reverberated so powerfully around me. Or drinking tea with Prince Sadruddin Aga Khan at his chateau overlooking Lake Geneva in 1991, talking about the Gulf War and what Jordan needed.

Then there was meeting Kathy Kelly, an American peace activist, pacifist and author, who was nominated for the Nobel Peace Prize, and Ghada Karmi, whose family left their home in Jerusalem in 1948 expecting to return after a few weeks. She has written wonderful books on being a Palestinian in the diaspora and on the history of Palestine.

General Amer Khammash of the Jordanian Armed Forces regaled me with tales of when he was with King Hussein and meeting with Gamal Abdel Nasser on the eve of the Six Day War.

My son sponsored Wendy Leach, an artist from New Zealand, to visit Jordan to paint various sites so we have a few of her lovely paintings, one of which is on the cover of this book.

I have been lucky to have experienced so many things, from watching the sun set over the Dead Sea with the twinkling lights of Jerusalem behind – so near and yet so far, and visiting the mysterious, magical Wadi Rum, which has appeared in many major films, to driving from Los Angeles to San Francisco in the late 1960s singing with gusto: *San Francisco* by Scott McKenzie. Sailing across Sydney Harbour and seeing the weird Opera House and the Bridge, experiencing the beauties of the North and South Islands of New Zealand or Glencoe's forbidding landscape and the battlefield at Culloden in Scotland.

13

Becoming an Activist

IN 1989 I WENT to a very interesting lecture by a Jordanian neurosurgeon who had just spent two and a half months on the West Bank. He talked about how he had been spending so much time dealing with appalling injuries, so many bullet wounds, fractured arms, beaten testicles, that he was never able to get on with routine medical matters. He talked about the use of rubber bullets, which, he explained, did the most enormous amount of damage. He talked about the problem of indiscipline among Palestinian youths, who weren't getting to school enough, and the psychological problems suffered by Israeli soldiers who were either becoming violent or were having problems of conscience. Those of us who lived in the Middle East always knew what was happening to the Palestinians, and how bad it was. We could also see that nobody in the West was interested in hearing that side of the story. Whereas countries like Kuwait had oil, which kept the West interested and eager to come to their rescue, the Palestinians had nothing that the West wanted.

In 1990, Saddam Hussein invaded Kuwait, and that was really when I, and many of my friends among the foreign wives, started to become activists and join protests. This group of women were a huge reason for me staying in Jordan for as long as I did. They were so supportive and such good friends – Americans, Brits, Bosnians, Germans, Jordanians and many other nationalities – even though, as a working woman, I couldn't always socialise as often as the others did. We would go down to the InterContinental hotel to talk to journalists and we were often shocked by the levels of ignorance they demonstrated about the history and politics of the area, particularly the people from US networks, who made up nonsense stories just to keep their bosses happy back in the States.

Although the invasion of Kuwait had taken everyone by surprise, His Majesty was confident that he could talk Saddam into withdrawing. He tried to keep everyone calm in the hope that the situation wouldn't escalate, but the Western media took that to mean he supported Saddam's actions and wrote the most scurrilous and inaccurate articles about him as a result. A group of us had been writing letters to heads of state, begging them to allow His Majesty time to negotiate with Saddam. It was the first time I fully appreciated just how blatantly journalists will lie in order to make their stories interesting to their readers. The *Daily Express* columnist, Jean Rook, was particularly vitriolic, calling His Majesty 'This ghastly little king'.

The following letter I wrote to my family at the time, shows just how strongly we felt about the situation.

> 'We are facing a crisis of a world gone mad' – King Hussein of Jordan
>
> I hope you will all understand that what we feel out here is probably very different to the feelings you have in the West. Having been involved with the media during the last month we can see how manipulative, distorted, inaccurate, untruthful and hysterical many members of the media can be. Amman is just bursting at the seams with the Western media rushing around en masse, looking for

stories – they are a story themselves. Some do try to find out what people really feel instead of writing what they think they should feel. Unfortunately, they are in the minority.

We have read the most amazing stories – Jean Rook should certainly never get near a Jordanian! Today newspapers did not just distort the truth about our press conference but actually lied. *Newsweek* slandered King Hussein – who knows what their motive was. I read one report in the *News of the World* which was just so unbelievable, pure fiction interlaced with some truth. Unfortunately, many read these stories, so as much as we would like to ignore their rubbish it is there, and to many people it is the truth. We saw the stories about the supposed rape of BA stewardesses splashed over the papers – which later proved to be quite untrue, but that, of course, was not headline news. We have also read emotive headlines – Saddam to starve foreign babies – it's alright for the West to starve Iraqi babies, I suppose? I could tell you a hundred stories about the press and how they get their stories. I am sure that they not only influence ordinary people's opinions but government opinions as well.

The hypocrisy and double standards of the West just leave us gasping. We have waited 23 years for the implementation of UN resolutions 242 and 338. The motives of the West are not on human terms at all; they are purely for their own self-interests. The Palestinian problem has never affected the West in the pocket so it has been brushed under the carpet. No matter that a whole population is being brutally and inhumanely used and their land occupied and annexed – the Palestinians are no threat to the economies of the West so their situation does not seem to justify the interest of the West to solve their problems.

For eight years Saddam Hussein was backed by the West in his war against Iran – where do you think he got his weapons from? The British have been very happy to do business with him. Now suddenly he is a terrible villain. Rightly or wrongly, to a vast majority of Arabs, Saddam Hussein is a symbol, someone who is at last standing up to the West and Israel after years of domination and injustice. The oil owning families of the Gulf and Saudi Arabia earned vast sums of money, which they spent with total abandon or invested in the Western economies, which not only damaged their reputations but earned the contempt of most ordinary Arabs. This does not justify the invasion of Kuwait but the West should try to understand the underlying reasons of the attitudes of many in this region.

Jordan is a sort of Arab democracy, so the only country where views can be freely expressed and, believe me, the country has never been so united.

The attacks on King Hussein have amazed and depressed us, just because the West thinks they are right only makes them right from their point of view. King Hussein has never failed to behave in a statesmanlike way, never wavered in his wish for a peaceful and diplomatic end to this terrible situation and staunchly upheld the view from the start that acquisition of territory by force is wrong.

The lack of understanding of Jordan by the West is what we should have expected but surely they should realise that Jordan's economy is in an extremely fragile state and to suddenly stop trading with Iraq is going to be catastrophic. Nearly 90 per cent of our oil comes from there, plus a large percentage of the economy is geared to trade with Iraq. It is not easy just to pull the plug at a moment's notice.

The complete disintegration of Arab unity is something to regret but we think that it is probably the leaders who disagree, not the people. I am sorry to say that the British have a lot to answer for as they have caused so many of the problems in this area. They arbitrarily carved up the region to suit their own interests. History is littered with their broken promises to the Arabs. Now many of the Arabs themselves have been corrupted by oil money and their dependence on the West – they are not without fault.

I hope Jordan can survive. At the moment the refugee problem is critical. We have thousands of people to feed and house when we can barely manage to look after ourselves. The international aid has been slow to move. It seems our allies desert us at the drop of a hat, we all feel so upset and bitter.

The Americans, and their allies, seem so confident that they can zap Iraq and reduce it to rubble, I hope they never try. Kuwait is not worth a war. President Bush and Mrs. Thatcher should not close doors, it seems they are out to get Saddam Hussein whatever the cost, to vilify him in every way possible, to accuse him of crimes that they themselves can be accused of. The US used chemical warfare (Agent Orange) in Vietnam. They misused and abused the indigenous population. They dropped the

> A-bomb on civilian targets in Japan. No country has an innocent history. The superpowers just push the pieces around to suit themselves and we are just the pawns, where will it all end?

Nobody writing outside Jordan took into account just how important the country's trade links with Iraq were and how hard our economy would be hit by any sanctions. I became so incensed by the whole thing that on one occasion I actually refused to shake hands with a *Daily Express* reporter.

Kate Adie did such an alarming report on the BBC about how there was no water in Amman and how the supermarket shelves were empty that my mother rang up to ask if I was all right. I had to remind her that there was always a shortage of water in Amman, because it was still only pumped once a week and the supermarket shelves would often be a little bare if there hadn't been goods delivered in a while.

One American guest told me how horrified he was at the thought of Saddam Hussein having nuclear weapons.

'Why are you not horrified that Israel has nuclear weapons?' I wanted to know.

'Well,' he said, 'Israel will only use theirs in a defensive way.'

'But if Saddam had them,' I pointed out, 'there is no way he could fire them at Israel without killing his brother Arabs.' To be clear, I do not think anyone should have nuclear weapons.

It's interesting that as early as 1984, I noted in my diary that the US president would never do anything to help the Arabs in an election year. As I marched for Gaza in 2024, I was very aware that the US was once more in an election year.

In 1991 we could hear the scud missiles going overhead as the Western ground forces started their campaign of 'shock and awe'. The wonderful Vanessa Redgrave came out on behalf of UNICEF and

I went to the Iraqi border with her in a helicopter. She has always spoken up for the Palestinians and her record for humanitarian work is second to none. I also flew to the border of Iraq with Prince Hassan and Princess Sarvath, for whom I was working, to show groups of journalists the size of the evacuee camps, filled as they were with over a million foreigners fleeing Iraq.

I had become an expert in planning and setting up these refugee camps, right down to details such as where to site the mobile toilets. Huge planes would then have to be chartered to fly the evacuees back to their home countries. I remember seeing one heading for Bangladesh, with its giant belly crammed full of people all squatting on the floor, with none of the usual comforts you would expect in an airliner, like seatbelts or even seats. It was an amazing feat to liaise with all the foreign governments and NGOs to get these people back to their home countries. The majority were Egyptian but there were Vietnamese, Bangladeshis, Sri Lankans and people from various other countries.

Later, we received four hundred Muslims from Bosnia who had been given sanctuary in Jordan and I became involved there too, as I had Bosnian friends. I was becoming increasingly aware of the gap between the big, altruistic gestures that political leaders made and the efforts of those on the ground, who actually had to implement the promises that had been made without consulting them. We managed to house the Bosnians in a couple of apartment blocks, but it cost an absolute fortune.

I was shocked by the sort of aid that would be sent by other countries. There was one country that sent medicines on the verge of expiring, but no instructions on how to use them in a language anyone could understand. Another sent shipments of rice which weren't fit for human consumption by the time they arrived. It would have been so much more effective if they had sent money, which could then have been spent in the local markets and circulated through the whole population. Some religious charities arrived with evangelical agendas and had to be sent packing. I was lucky enough to go to Geneva with the secretary-general of the Ministry of the Interior to put the case to the International Committee of the Red Cross (ICRC) and other agencies and we were invited to meet with Prince Sadruddin Aga Khan at his beautiful Chateau de Bellerive overlooking Lake Geneva.

I may have been naive about the Middle East when I arrived there at the age of twenty-one, but I was now beginning to understand only too well what was happening and how big a role the UK and the USA had played in stoking and spreading the chaos.

14

Women and Children

SO, LIFE WENT ON and in the 1990s I got myself involved in various projects that just seemed to come my way. I visited two women's prisons, wanting to set up projects to help the prisoners. There were detainees under the rule of 'administrative detention', women incarcerated for being victims of attempted or proposed 'honour' killings. I always hated that term, because these crimes are murder, just like every other kind of deliberate killing. 'Honour', I felt, had nothing to do with it. I will never forget the eyes of one woman I met, whose brother had shot her seven times. She had survived all those bullets and now she was the one being held in detention, as if she were the one who had committed the crime. There were still a lot of these killings happening in Jordan and often the other women of the family were complicit in the crimes, getting their youngest sons to perform the actual murders. They could then drop the charges, as they were the families of both the victims and the perpetrators, and because the boys were young they would go unpunished. The laws have been changed after many years of lobbying (a male-dominated parliament didn't help the process at all), though these crimes still occur much too often.

I was surprised how clean the prisons were, although I still wouldn't have wanted to be imprisoned in there myself. We managed to set up training courses so that even the women who were illiterate could learn trades like hairdressing and embroidery while they were incarcerated. One female prisoner I met was in jail for murdering her husband.

'It must have been domestic violence that drove her to do it,' I suggested to the accompanying police officer.

'No,' she said, 'You have got it all wrong. Her husband had gone to work in another Arab country and he had left a male relative to look after his wife and children. The wife had an affair with that relative and when the husband returned for a vacation, she smothered him while he was sleeping.' I realised that I should be careful never to jump to conclusions.

Wanting to find out more, I was able to accompany some British police officers on official visits that had been arranged for them to various Jordanian prisons. I was chatting happily with one male prisoner, who seemed very pleasant and humorous, until we were told he had poisoned both his children with cyanide because he was jealous of the amount of time and attention they were getting from his wife, their mother.

I was often moved by the stories the prisoners told me, so much so that the governor of one prison said, 'Umm Muwaffaq, you must not be fooled into believing everything these people say to you.' I dare say I was sometimes naive and overly gullible, but that didn't seem a good reason not to continue trying to improve conditions for all concerned.

Some of the women who were brought into the prisons were prostitutes and I could see that many of them needed treatment for sexually transmitted infections. I would say almost none of them had chosen the profession voluntarily. There was one very respectable Iraqi family who had fled Iraq and fallen on such hard times that they had prostituted their very young daughters in order to get some money to eat. I was so moved by their plight that I thought there must be some way to help people in that position. I worked closely with my friend, Dr Muhammed al-Hadid, a Bedouin, who was Head of the Jordan Red

Crescent (the Muslim version of the Red Cross) and Prince Hassan supported me to travel to the UK to see how sexual health clinics were run there.

Muhammed was a wonderful friend over many years. When my son was buying me an apartment in Amman, he was 10,000 dinars short of the money we needed to secure it. I am never comfortable borrowing money from anyone, but I liked this apartment and we were going to lose it if we couldn't come up with the deposit in time. I went to see Muhammed. Bedouin people are renowned for their generosity and I had done a lot of work with him by then.

'I hate to ask you this,' I said, 'but you are the only person I know who I can ask. I just need to borrow 10,000 dinars for a week.'

'Do you want it tonight or tomorrow morning?' he asked, without batting an eyelid. It was pure Bedouin generosity and I was so grateful. We were able to buy the apartment and Muwaffaq paid him back a week later.

I also suggested to Muhammed that we might invite Oxfam to open some shops around Jordan. They sent out a fascinating man, called Andrew, who explained to me how the whole process worked. We collected a load of stuff in a Red Crescent warehouse, but I couldn't handle it all on my own and my Arabic wasn't good enough either, so the project petered out.

I also became involved in the problem of drug abuse in the city. I had personal experience of this because a member of the family became a victim of the drug culture and finally overdosed on heroin. He had travelled to England to study and I think that was where he first became involved, being a little unstable anyway. The family begged me to go to the police to get him arrested because they didn't feel safe and they knew that I had good contacts there. It was heartbreaking seeing this man destroying his family. He had been jailed many times and when he came out of prison for the last time, he pleaded with his sister for

40 dinars to go out and buy something. She gave him the money and he immediately bought heroin which he injected into his arm and died immediately. To see him sitting there, dead, with the needle still in his arm, brought home to me how drugs not only destroy the lives of the victims but also those who are close to them. They were very ashamed to have a drug addict in the family and had no idea how to manage the situation. Prince Hassan supported me to go on another trip to England to study how drug rehabilitation worked there.

The main problem for Jordan is that it is geographically at the centre of a number of drug routes, particularly into Israel, where they consume a lot of recreational substances. The Public Security Department had a rehabilitation centre at the top of one of the jebels with the rule that if you came in voluntarily, you wouldn't be given a prison record, which I thought was very civilised. I believe Jordan had the only police force in the world who actually ran rehab for drug abusers, and I was taken to see the furnaces where they burned everything that the Drug Enforcement Agency had managed to seize. It had an unforgettable aroma! The government wanted to build a bigger rehabilitation facility in the scenic, wooded area up north, which would have meant the destruction of a lot of trees. I was very keen not to do that and travelled around with a wonderful police officer, Fadel, who had previously worked at the Drug Enforcement Agency, until we found a beautiful area in the municipality, which had no trees in it. The initial plan was for one large building, but I thought something on a more human scale, with cloisters and gardens, would be more effective for treatment. The building was commissioned and built, and I was very happy with the result.

In September 1994 I also read an article in *The Independent* newspaper about sexual attacks on English women abroad, which set me off on another mission. One of the women they talked to was a British–Iraqi woman who had been raped in Jordan and treated very badly by the authorities when she reported it. I had experienced two incidents of sexual assault in Jordan myself, in the 1980s. One time I was on my way to a friend's house for lunch when a man walking directly towards me suddenly grabbed my breasts. I shrieked and he ran off. I ran after him, shouting, 'stop him!' but I couldn't keep up and nobody else came to my aid. Another time, I was in the sea when a man swam over and grabbed me between the legs. Again, my screams scared him off and by the time I had got out of the water he had disappeared. Neither of these incidents were serious, but they helped me to understand how it felt and to empathise with women who were in more vulnerable situations than I was.

I asked Prince Hassan and Princess Sarvath if I could do something about the British–Iraqi woman. They agreed and I went to the British embassy to find out exactly what had happened. They told me that the police had arrested the perpetrator, who was the Egyptian caretaker in the block of flats where she was staying. The police, however, had asked her a lot of personal questions, which implied that she had been 'asking for it'. I suggested that the embassy set up a project to train the police in the correct way to handle these sorts of crimes and in how to interview rape victims sympathetically. They agreed that it was a good idea and a few months later a UK police team came out to assess our police procedures for rape and sexual assault. I took them around to talk to the police, and into prisons, which they had to admit were better than their equivalents in the UK. We got the go-ahead to set up some courses and they sent out Sergeant Carol Woodcock of the Lancashire Constabulary, who was wonderful. We decided not to call her 'Sergeant' because in Jordan that would give her a very low status, so she was addressed as 'Inspector'. She and I talked a lot and she explained how family protection units work in the UK. This led to me wanting to do something about child abuse in Jordan as well, but I was surprised by how many people, when I spoke to them about it, assured me that there was 'no such thing'. I would explain that every country in the world suffers from child abuse, that it is just kept secret, but there was enormous resistance to the suggestion that there was even a problem. It took a long time and much consultation to find an appropriate name for this fledgling unit, but we decided on Family Protection Unit which then became Family Protection Department.

We set up a small sexual assault unit to start with and they put a police officer in charge who had a degree in sociology, which made me furious because I wanted rape and assault to be seen as crimes only just below murder, to be investigated by fully-fledged detectives, not social workers. I felt very strongly that the whole process should be about protecting the safety and confidentiality of the victims. Everything was meant to be anonymous, but this officer would even bring his children into sessions. I also thought the whole overall project should be run by the police, and not by the Ministry of Social Development, because the police are always there, providing continuity, whereas ministers come and go and political agendas change with them. The Prince and Princess came to see what was happening, along with the Head of Intelligence, who I knew well. The man in charge then made a fool of himself and they replaced him with Lieutenant-Colonel Fadel al-Hmoud, the person I had wanted all along, who stayed in the role for many years and did a great job of professionalising the process. He is now a senator in the Upper House of Parliament. It was important that the unit was there to serve the community, not simply to showcase its own importance and the importance of the people running it.

We initially included domestic violence in the brief as well, but that became chaotic because whenever women came to report abuse, their whole families would also turn up, shouting and screaming at one another, and the original complainant would then be intimidated, drop the charges and go home to face further abuse. So, we concentrated our efforts on child abuse and sexual abuse. I was surprised by the level of ignorance about sexual matters among the female police officers we were recruiting. They didn't know any of the terms they would need if they were questioning someone, let alone all the things that can happen to an abuse victim. It was important to me that we didn't try to impose the British way of thinking onto them, but that we listened closely to them in order to find out what they needed and wanted, so that we could then look for ways to provide it. One of the policewomen I interviewed in 1998 became a lifelong friend. Taghreed came from a disadvantaged background, living in the north of Jordan. She got to university and studied English Literature and then joined the police. Her English was so good that it was easy for me to talk to her and exchange ideas. She managed to get a Chevening scholarship to do a master's degree in the UK and got a Master of Laws in Human Rights, with distinction. I then persuaded her to go for a PhD with a Fulbright scholarship, which she did and was accepted, but unfortunately the director of the Public Security Department would not allow her to go. I was so annoyed but could not get him to change his mind. The following year a new director was appointed, Tahseen Shurdom, who was a pal of mine so he said to me, 'I cannot say no to you Trisha!' So, Taghreed got her PhD in the USA and also gave birth to two sons. She retired from the police and I was very sad that Jordan didn't make more use of her talents, but she is now the Family Care Authority director-general-advisor to the government of Abu Dhabi. From a little village in the far north of Jordan to a PhD and a great job in the Gulf.

The project had to be expanded beyond just a police department because it was important to involve the Ministry of Justice, the Ministry of Health and the Ministry of Social Development. The whole project ended up costing £ 2.5 million, all provided by the British government. As with all aid, a large proportion of the money went into employing British consultants, including paying for their flights and accommodation. Fadel and I, as well as a few other officers, went on another educational visit to the UK, where we met the Chief Constable of Gloucestershire, Tony Butler. I asked him if he could come out to Jordan to help with training and the courts, which he did. He was extremely helpful and became a good friend in the process. I became totally immersed in the whole project and it felt like a genuinely worthwhile thing to do.

The mayor of Amman's father had been a pilot with my husband. He was now the person who settled disputes among the Bedouin tribes. I went to see him and asked if he would ask his son if we could have some land for the police to set up the Family Protection Department. He came up trumps and the police were given a very nice piece of land to build on. We then went on to set up units around the country. I gave them the ancient Mercedes the King had given me when I came back to Jordan and bought myself a Honda four-wheel drive.

When I received an OBE for 'Services to Women and Children's Rights in the Middle East' it felt as if I wasn't alone and that there were others who appreciated how useful all the work had been. The police chief, who had been antagonistic towards me at the beginning, eventually told me that whereas he had initially thought I was just doing it for my own fame and aggrandisement, he had now changed his mind. He, too, then became a good friend.

I had no idea I was up for the award. The first I knew was when the British ambassador asked me down to his residence. His wife was away somewhere, so it was just the two of us and as we chatted over a cup of tea, he handed me a very stiff envelope. When I opened it, it was from Buckingham Palace, asking if I would accept an OBE.

I assured him I was deeply flattered and happy to accept.

'But you can't tell anybody,' he warned me.

'Not even my son?'

'Well, perhaps,' he grinned, 'as long as you swear him to secrecy.'

I rang Muwaffaq in Singapore, where he was working, and I could tell he was shocked by the news. I don't think children ever really take in what their parents are doing or how they are regarded by the wider world.

I was allowed to take three guests to the investiture at Buckingham Palace, which was hard as I had two sisters and I also wanted to take my mother and my son. So, in the end I asked my mother, my son and Mum's only granddaughter, Helen. Mum then hosted us all to go to Cliveden for a big tea with all my friends. I received the award from Prince Charles, as he then was, which was a very nice experience.

When my nephew was studying at Cambridge University my mother and I drove up to see him. We passed a village called Braybrooke (my maiden name) and decided to go and have a look and to our amazement a river called Jordan flowed through it!

15

The Death of the King

WHEN JORDAN SIGNED THE peace treaty with Israel in October 1994, I had a very aggressive late-night call from an Israeli television network, telling me that they had heard I was trying to make contact with the pilot who had shot Muwaffaq down and asking if I would do an interview with him. I could hardly contain my emotions but managed politely to say that I had absolutely no wish to meet this pilot and was not interested in doing any interview. I had no intention of allowing myself, and Muwaffaq's memory, to be used as Israeli propaganda. After hanging up, I cried all night. The network approached me again a few months later through other people and I asked the Palace to put a stop to it because I was never going to change my mind. I wondered what the motives were behind these attempts to contact me. I have no doubt that peace is the only way to go, but that does not mean that I have to be friends with Israelis. I believe that they stole a country that did not belong to them. They exist there now and we have to recognise this fact, but we do not have to agree with their policies just because they exist.

The peace treaty meant that there were a lot more Israeli visitors around Jordan. Everyone in the country was trying to build hotels to take advantage of this boom in the tourist trade, with little thought to the long-term consequences for the environment. Petra had become almost unrecognisable, with masses of hotels being built on the hillsides overlooking Wadi Araba, just eight kilometres away. Gerald Durrell called tourism 'the plague' and I think he was right. The one good thing about the Gulf War was that all the tourists disappeared for a while! Though of course, this not good for the local people who lost their incomes.

It was a shock when the Israeli prime minister, Yitzhak Rabin, was assassinated in 1995, although not too many Palestinians wept for his loss after his 'break their bones' policy. It was a relief to discover the assassin was an Israeli and not an Arab, because that could easily have led us back to war. It was a terrible lapse in security and a sad loss to the peace process. He was a strong man and I believe that with his tough background, his change to believing in peace could have carried most of the Israeli people with him.

When the King became fatally ill in 1999 at only sixty-three years old, he named his son, Abdullah, as the new crown prince and his heir, in order to keep the throne in his direct line. This meant he was replacing his brother, Prince Hassan, whom I was working for. Prince Hassan had been named as the crown prince when Abdullah was still a small child, but now Abdullah was a man in his mid-thirties. The King actually told his son, 'I chose you to be king because I knew you didn't want it.' I guess he believed he could rely on Abdullah to have the country's interests at heart and keep the line of succession through his own children.

This sudden demotion must have been a shattering blow for Prince Hassan and his family, because he was devoted to his country and worked so hard in every way, but I have to admit my first thought on hearing the news was for myself. Did this mean I was going to be out of a job? How, I wondered, was I going to support myself if Prince Hassan no longer needed my services? I was already making enquiries among my network of friends about possible jobs when I got a phone call from the military assistant, asking if I was coming into the Office of the Crown Prince that day. I told him that I didn't think so.

'Prince Hassan wants to talk to everyone who is leaving the Office,' he said.

'Oh, so I am one of the ones leaving the Office?'

'Yes.'

I was deeply upset to be informed of my dismissal in this manner and went up to the office, where I was told that I was going to be kept on after all. The uncomfortable situation dragged on for a year. I knew that Queen Rania was interested in child abuse, so when the Hassans were away on a visit to Morocco, I went to chat with her and asked if I could bring the project to her, if Prince Hassan agreed.

'Yes,' she said, 'I wanted to ask, but I didn't want to upset the Hassans.'

When the Hassans came back from Morocco I thought of writing them a letter, explaining what I had done, but a friend pointed out that was a coward's way out. So, I asked for a face-to-face meeting. Someone, however, had already told them about my plans, so I didn't actually see them to explain. I was very truthful about what had happened, but it would have been better if I had lied. They must have already been hurting and feeling betrayed, because Prince Hassan had lived his life believing that he was next in line to the throne and suddenly he found he was removed from that position. Now, they thought I had betrayed them as well and they were not happy with me. I could see that I had not handled the situation well at all. I became so stressed that I thought I was having a heart attack and went to see the doctor. He checked my heart and reassured me that if I ever had a heart attack, he would leave medicine.

'It is an anxiety attack,' he told me.

The King's death hit me, and many Jordanians, very hard. Standing with another English friend, watching his coffin go by in the red

Land-Rover, we both wept genuine tears. Virtually every world leader of the time came to pay their respects that day.

By then I was in my late fifties and Queen Rania's team really didn't want some interfering old white woman in the Queen's Office. I could understand their point of view. I was now a fish out of water, so I stepped aside after being told I had to leave and instead continued to work with Fadel and the police.

By that stage Muwaffaq had started to be very successful in the oil trading world and was able to help me financially, so I was less worried about my future. The first time he gave me some money, at the end of the 1990s, I went straight into a supermarket in Amman and bought myself some bacon and strawberries, two luxuries I had been avoiding buying for years, purely for budgetary reasons.

In 2003, the West attacked Iraq again. Looking at my diaries from the time, I see that I also noted that, 'meanwhile Israelis are killing five or six Palestinians a day, breaking all human rights laws, international laws and Geneva conventions, and no one says a dickie bird.'

So, life continued, but now I had time for socialising with friends while also keeping up with what was happening in the Family Protection Department.

16

Discoveries in the Dead Sea

IN 2009 I RECEIVED an email from Dr Gideon Hadas, an Israeli archaeologist, who had managed to find my address online. He informed me that he was Director of the Ein Gedi Oasis Excavations archaeological delegation. In the course of their explorations, he told me, they had found some remains of a Jordanian Hunter jet north of Ein Gedi, on what in the 1960s would have been the waterline of the Dead Sea. He offered to escort me to the site if I would like that. I sent the email to Muwaffaq because, although I didn't want to go, I thought he might and, if so, I would have gone with him. He said he didn't want to go either. I then started asking every influential contact I had, to see if we could get some of the remains brought back for our air force museum.

A year later Gideon wrote to me again, saying, 'As you know, the remains of your husband's plane were returned to Jordan today at the Allenby Bridge. I was very disappointed not to meet you there, but if you come to Israel, I would be very glad to meet you.'

I was furious. The air force and the army only knew about the discovery because I had told them, the least they could have done was inform me that the ceremony was happening. I was so upset because it seemed to epitomise the way that all women were treated in that part of the world, being completely discounted. I made a phone call and was told it had been the army who had arranged the event. I demanded that they send me a piece of the aircraft and that evening a piece of undercarriage arrived in a cardboard box. The rest went into the museum.

I had begun to think about returning to England now that I was in my sixties and this incident made my mind up for me. In 2009 I packed up everything and headed to Poole, in Dorset, where my mother and youngest sister were still living.

Muwaffaq and his wonderful wife, Angel, had moved to London with my two granddaughters, Maia and Kiri. They had met in Singapore where Angel was working in hospitality. Muwaffaq was now a senior oil trader at the bank where he worked in London and they were living in a flat in St John's Wood.

I rented a few different flats in Poole, but when Mum died, Muwaffaq suggested I come up to London to be close to him and his family. I readily agreed and he very generously bought an apartment for me to live in, in Maida Vale, which is just a few minutes' walk from St John's Wood.

They remained in London for about seven years, during which time Muwaffaq set up his own company, before moving back to Singapore, close to Angel's family. I never really settled in Maida Vale (although it was a lovely flat), feeling rather lonely in a block that seemed deserted during the day, and so I moved south of the river to a house in Barnes, an area which I felt had more community spirit and where I am very happy.

I made a few trips out to Singapore, but they weren't terribly successful because Muwaffaq and Angel were busy with their work and their lives, the girls were at school and I got very bored. It was difficult and I probably wasn't always as tactful as I should have been. Angel did her best, but Muwaffaq was not happy and there were some emotional and upsetting moments. I went for therapy to try and sort out my feelings and that helped a lot, confirming that I needed to stand up for myself more. I had had the same problem with my relationship with my mother, never speaking my mind and sulking instead, while she was able to flare up and get everything out of her system. I have never been good at confrontation.

My relationship with Muwaffaq now is the best it has ever been and he is never anything other than generous in his financial support for me. Without him I would be in a bit of a mess, since I have no pension. Not that I would have wanted to miss out on any of my adventures in life simply in order to have a pension now, but my old age would have been a struggle if I had continued trying to fund myself.

On my trips to Singapore, I would then travel on to New Zealand to stay with my friend, Ginny, who was nanny to King Hussein's twin daughters when they were very small. She married Tuma from Jerusalem and had three boys, eventually moving to Auckland. I'm glad I made those trips when I did, because once Covid struck in 2020, travelling to Singapore became out of the question.

Many years after our last conversation, Gideon Hadas came back to me again, to tell me they had found a broken plaque in the desert, commemorating Muwaffaq in Arabic, which he had repaired and attached to a stone boulder, together with a Hebrew plaque describing the events of 13 November 1966. It was very welcome news because it meant that Muwaffaq's name will never be forgotten, even after I have gone, even after our son and grandchildren have gone.

I had sixteen months of marriage, four of which I spent in the UK and six of which I was pregnant and felt ill, so I am hardly an expert on marriage and how it works. Does marrying someone from another religion, race and culture make it more challenging? And do the children of mixed marriages suffer? In 1965, when I was walking in Wolverhampton with my husband, everyone stared because he was so dark-skinned and when I was walking in Amman everyone stared because I was white-skinned! In Jordan, if you were not Arab, you were a foreigner, and that never changed, as you could not fully integrate. It is hard work to conform to what we think our husbands and their families want us to be. If anything bad happens in the marriage, the 'foreigner' is likely to want to be with her own culture and family. It is difficult to manage on one's own. It is about give and take, I suppose, like any marriage anywhere, but there are extra demands when learning how to adapt. It is undoubtedly different being married to a Muslim rather than to a Christian. But then there is the plus side to marrying into another culture, allowing us to see that we are all citizens of the world, albeit with different perspectives and different beliefs, and to be immersed into a wonderful culture that few people in the West are aware of.

My grandchildren are a quarter Chinese, a quarter Indian, a quarter Arab and a quarter British; hopefully this impacts on their lives positively.

The two worst days in my life were when my husband was killed and when my son told me on FaceTime, 'Mum, I have cancer.' I wished it had been me instead of him. He decided that his diagnosis was something he would share with everyone and I believe that the love and support that came back really helped him. He was treated by the best and the prognosis is now good. We just hope and pray it won't come back. In the meantime, he and Angel have settled Maia and Kiri in university, one in LA and the other in New York, and they are now travelling and having fun. Recently, Maia got an Uber and the driver was a Jordanian, who, when he heard her name, gave her a lesson about her grandfather!

17

A Return Trip

On 5 June 2024, fifty-five years after the Six Day War, sixty years and one month after I first set foot in Jordan and seven years since I had last visited, I returned, because I heard that my husband's number two in the Battle of Samu, Ihsan Shurdom, was dying.

Many things have changed since I was last there. I had been living in London all through the Covid pandemic, while Muwaffaq, Angel and my grandchildren had been making their lives in Singapore. Developments in technology have meant that I have been closely linked to them by screens and typed messages, but I have still been living nearly 7,000 physical miles away from them.

The attack by Hamas upon Israel, and Israel's ferocious response in Gaza, has now polarised world opinion and opened the eyes of many to how greatly the Palestinians have been suffering over the last seventy to eighty years. Like many people in Europe at the time, when I first went to Jordan, I knew virtually nothing about the Middle East; now, stories from the area are on the world's screens nightly. Sixty years ago, I drove out to Jordan, knowing nothing, but now I know a great deal and have lived through more than half a century with the Jordanian people. I looked forward to revisiting many familiar sights, sounds and scents, but I also expected to find things changed in many ways by recent events.

Once more I boarded a plane for Amman with a sense of anticipation. I knew the captain of the aircraft, who used to be a helicopter pilot in the RJAF, and two other passengers, so the trip already felt like coming home. As I had hoped, my arrival brought back so many memories, as well as some surprises. The reasonably efficient and modern airport immediately reminded me of the Arab side of the country's culture, with boisterous shouting, drums and bagpipes greeting some of the arriving passengers, welcoming them to the Kingdom. Being driven into the bright lights of the city from the airport at midnight, I could see clearly how much had changed in the country, which had a population of one million when I first arrived in 1964 and was now home to over eleven million. The traffic jams and driving habits seemed even worse than in 1964, the streets crammed with so many cars that it took an age to get anywhere.

I stayed with my wonderful pals, Karen (an American widow of a Jordanian) and Marian (British and married to an Armenian–Jordanian), during the visit and Ihsan died four days after my arrival. He was buried the next day, as is the custom, and I felt that the last string connecting me to my beloved husband had finally been cut.

After Ihsan's funeral there was the traditional Azaa', where people come to give their condolences and pay their respects, so I went to the Circassian hall twice and met many of the women I have known for years. I saw his widow, Margaret, a few times while I was there. She has been a pal for many years and I felt for her sorrow. We share so many memories, both good and bad. We have been through so much together.

Now, of course, the eyes of the world are on Israel once more, as it continues to raze Gaza to the ground, behaving with exactly the same cruel and ruthless violence that all of us in Amman have learned to expect. It seems that the killing and plundering will never end.

While I was in Amman, I visited Muwaffaq's grave, in the royal cemetery inside the palace grounds, accompanied by the wonderful Prince Raad and Princess Majda (who, sadly, recently died), as well as my friend Karen. It was so emotional, remembering back to the day when the air force Land-Rover took the young, pregnant me up for the burial after my husband's coffin had been paraded through the streets of Amman, the day when all my dreams were shattered and I had to start my life again.

Ever since that day I have been filled with the fear that when someone leaves, I will never see them again.

We all have sorrows in our lives, but war is the most terrible of all. I will never understand why so many people feel they have to kill each other.

Acknowledgements

This has been such an interesting experience – delving into my life and adventures. What to put in and what to leave out! I hope my granddaughters enjoy reading about what their Teta got up to.

My heartfelt thanks and love to Muwaffaq and Angel. To Maia and Kiri, may your lives be full of joy and happiness though there will surely be bumps along the way. Stay tall and be kind.

To King Hussein, who loved his pilots and helped and supported me through the years. Prince Hassan and Princess Sarvath – I really enjoyed working for them both on a variety of projects from weddings to family protection and drug rehabilitation to number just a few. Prince Zeid bin Shaker and his wife Nawzat, a lovely couple – I would never have met the wonderful Michael Parker if I had not been working for them.

To the pals I have around the world but especially in Jordan, too many to name but I cherish each and every one. All of them have a story to tell.

To my sisters, Jill and Ann and their families. We have trodden different paths, but are still family.

Thank you Andrew Crofts for putting this all together. A pleasure to work with you. Thank you also to Whitefox for steering me through the publishing maze and to Wendy Leach for the painting on the cover. Thank you to my wonderful pal Jacky for her help and support throughout the process.

To all those in the Middle East who strive for peace, dignity and justice.

Patricia (Trisha) Salti's life, guided by chance, fluke and serendipity, unfolded in the vibrant heart of the Middle East, a land steeped in history and culture, where she spent forty-one remarkable years. There, she experienced happiness, tragedy, wars, amazing jobs and adventures and an insight into the lives and traditions of those living in Jordan.

She returned to the United Kingdom in 2009, but Jordan remains deeply rooted in her heart, along with cherished memories of a life immersed in its rich history and culture. The close-knit circle of friends who supported her through so much, as well as her Jordanian family and friends, shared their traditions and introduced her to the exquisite cuisine of the Middle East. She feels profoundly lucky to have lived a life that offered her so much.

In 2002, Patricia was awarded an OBE for services to women and children's rights in the Middle East.

www.ingramcontent.com/pod-product-compliance
Lightning Source LLC
Chambersburg PA
CBHW071204070526
44584CB00019B/2913